RUSSIA

KAZAKHSTAN

MONGOLIA

Heilongjiang

KYRGYZSTAN

Jilin

Xinjiang

Liaoning

TAJIKISTAN

Nei Mengu (Inner Mongolia)

⊛Beijing
3 2 1
4

NORTH
KOREA

AFGHANISTAN

PAKISTAN

C H I N A

Shanxi

Hebei
5 6
7

Tianjin

SOUTH
KOREA

Qinghai

Ningxia

Shandong

Yellow Sea

Huang He (Yellow River)

8

Gansu

Shaanxi

Henan

Jiangsu
14

Anhui

15
13 12

13

Shanghai

Xixang
(Tibet)

Hubei

NEPAL

9 10
11

Chongqing

16 18
Zhejiang
17

20

East China Sea

Sichuan

Chang Jiang (Yangzi River)

Jiangxi

20
19

Fujian

Hunan

Guizhou

Taiwan

Yunnan

Guangxi

21

Guangdong

N

VIETNAM

Hainan

Hong
Kong

LAOS

South
China
Sea

PHILIPPINES

THAILAND

0 50 100   200   300   400   500
miles

0 50 100 200 300 400 500
kilometers

KEY

1 **Bridges of the Forbidden City**
   Beijing

2 **Sea Palace Bridges**
   Beijing

3 **"Garden of Gardens" Bridges**
   Beijing

4 **Lugou Bridge**
   Wanping, Beijing

5 **Zhaozhou Bridge**
   Zhaoxian, Hebei

6 **Dulin Bridge and Shan Bridge**
   Cangzhou, Hebei

7 **Jingxing Bridge**
   Cangyan Mountains, Hebei

8 **Baling Bridge**
   Weiyuan, Gansu

9 **Hongjun Bridge**
   Qinglinkou, Sichuan

10 **Jiemei Bridges**
   Anxian, Sichuan

11 **Anlan Suspension Bridge**
   Dujiangyan, Guanxian, Sichuan

12 **Bridges in the Lower Yangzi Watertowns**
   Jiangsu, Shanghai, and Zhejiang

13 **Suzhou and Hangzhou Garden Bridges**
   Jiangsu and Zhejiang

14 **Wuting Bridge**
   Yangzhou, Jiangsu

15 **Baodai Bridge**
   Suzhou, Jiangsu

16 **Huizhou Covered Bridges**
   Anhui and Jiangxi

17 **Caihong Bridge**
   Wuyuan, Jiangxi

18 **Bei'an Bridge**
   Shexian, Anhui

19 **Megalithic Stone Beam Bridges**
   Quanzhou, Fujian

20 **Covered Wooden Bridges**
   Southern Zhejiang and Northern Fujian

21 **Dong "Wind-and-Rain" Bridges**
   Sanjiang, Guangxi

Chinese Bridges

Living Architecture From China's Past

Ronald G. Knapp

Photography by
A. Chester Ong

Foreword by Peter Bol

TUTTLE PUBLISHING
Tokyo • Rutland, Vermont • Singapore

Published by Tuttle Publishing, an imprint of
Periplus Editions (HK) Ltd, with editorial offices
at 61 Tai Seng Avenue #02-12, Singapore 534167.

Text © 2008 Ronald G. Knapp
Photographs © 2008 A. Chester Ong and Periplus
Editions (HK) Ltd.

Library of Congress Control Number 2008923152
ISBN 978-0-8048-3884-9

Distributed by:
North America, Latin America & Europe
Tuttle Publishing
364 Innovation Drive,
North Clarendon, VT 05759-9436 U.S.A.
Tel: 1 (802) 773-8930; Fax: 1 (802) 773-6993
info@tuttlepublishing.com
www.tuttlepublishing.com

Asia Pacific
Berkeley Books Pte Ltd
61 Tai Seng Avenue
#02-12, Singapore 534167.
Tel: (65) 6280 1330; Fax: (65) 6280 6290
inquiries@periplus.com.sg
www.periplus.com

Printed in Singapore
11 10 09 08
6 5 4 3 2 1

TUTTLE PUBLISHING® is a registered
trademark of Tuttle Publishing, a division of
Periplus Editions (HK) Ltd.

Front endpaper:
The emperor's entourage passes over a high
single-arch bridge spanning a rushing stream in
the foothills of Mount Tai near Kaishan Temple,
Shandong province. Wang Hui and assistants,
*The Kangxi Emperor's Southern Tour, Scroll Three:
Ji'nan to Mount Tai,* Qing dynasty, handscroll, ink
and color on silk. © Metropolitan Museum of Art,
New York.

Back endpaper:
*Zhaozhou Stone Bridge With Baxian [Eight Im-
mortals], Lu Ban, and Others Crossing It,* ca. 2000,
woodcut on paper. Samuel Dorsky Museum of
Art, State University of New York at New Paltz.

Page 1:
The Yudai (Jade Belt) Bridge, a steep single-arch
humpbacked bridge built in 1750, is one of six
spans along the western causeway in the Yihe
Yuan or Summer Palace, Beijing.

Page 2:
Constructed in the thirteenth century during
the Yuan dynasty in what is today Beihai Park,
the Yong'an (Eternal Peace) Bridge is a low triple-
arch structure leading through the Duiyun (Piled-
up Clouds) Arch to Qionghua Islet.

Pages 4–5:
Masked by a modern arched bridge in the craggy
Cangyan Mountains of western Hebei province is
the Qiaolou Hall, a temple perched on the spanning Jingxing Bridge.

Page 6:
In the rugged mountains of northwestern Fujian
province, covered bridges such as the 42.5-meter-
long Yangmeizhou Bridge in Shouning county,
have been important links in regional trade since
at least the eighteenth century.

CONTENTS

FOREWORD

Crossing a bridge today—eyes on the traffic and mind already on the other side—it is too easy to pass over the span without reflecting on its engineering, its aesthetics, and its history. With their studies of the diverse traditions of bridge building, the "wind-and-rain" bridges of Guangxi, the white marble stonework of imperial bridges in the capital, the soaring covered bridges of southern Zhejiang, author Ronald Knapp and photographer Chester Ong have created a book that shows us how to pay attention. Like so many others who have become interested in material culture and local society, I have learned to look forward to Ron Knapp's next book on Chinese vernacular architecture. *Chinese Bridges* is a worthy successor to his previous work in this series, *Chinese Houses*.

Bridges are good metaphors. They join what is separated; they increase communication; they facilitate circulation; they are social and cultural constructions. The vernacular architecture of China is a visual bridge to the social and political worlds out of which it emerged. Bridges are anchored to the valley walls and the streambeds they traverse, and they are also anchored in the communities that build them. Even today, when local government is responsible for the infrastructure of travel, it is not hard to find rural towns where bridges are built by collecting donations from the residents. I remember the stone stele that recorded the gifts of five and ten yuan that paid for the most basic of bridges, the rough granite slabs that bridged the stream dividing a village in the mountains of Zhejiang's Dongyang. I am not sure that it was the size of the donation that required the stele, although it was a time and place when even a few yuan were of consequence; rather, it was the fact of a shared, and successful, communal endeavor that was being celebrated.

Slabs across a stream can facilitate community building. The merchants displaying their wares in the famous depiction of Song-dynasty Kaifeng's rainbow bridge were going where the people were. But many of the covered bridges we see here were also built as public spaces, attracting people to gather in the comfortable shade, cooled by the breezes sweeping over the summer river. Often they were religious sites as well. Obviously, bridge shrines asked gods to protect the bridge, but sometimes these shrines—a bridge being a well-trafficked spot—brought worshippers to the deity. Not a few bridges were also teahouses. The county towns of Yongkang and Wuyi in Zhejiang have restored their old covered bridges to great effect. Walking across I have found myself among the relaxing crowds—of old men playing cards, of families with children, of musicians with their instruments—and there were even a few people who were simply trying to cross the river.

Today, many old bridges have become architectural monuments. Consider the arching covered bridges in Taishun, amply illustrated in this volume, in the hill country along the Zhejiang-Fujian border, an area I know well. These are not quite bridges to nowhere—we can still see that they were once nodes in the networks of narrow imperial highways—but the modern road system has made the old roads and bridges far less relevant. Looking down to the riverbed, I see the marks of old foundations; the current bridge seems to be the third or fourth incarnation of a bridge at this spot. Historians tell us that many of these elegant bridges were built by lineages not for their own travel but as an investment: a more convenient bridge could shift trade routes through their villages, to their profit. Villages and roads come and go, and so do bridges.

And that brings us to the problem of preservation. The aesthetics of many bridges justifies their preservation, however impractical they have become. It ought to be obvious that aesthetic goals figured centrally in the construction of these bridges in the first place. The are works of art and engineering. Many of the bridges depicted in this volume will be preserved, restored today as a memory of the past rather than for their practical utility. But many that are not here will be lost. This volume should inspire us, as we travel through China, to look for bridges, to photograph them, to draw attention to them, and perhaps to help preserve them.

Peter Bol
Harvard University

Part One

CHINA'S ANCIENT BRIDGE BUILDING TRADITIONS

ARCHITECTURE OVER WATER

Unlike palaces and temples—even houses—that are noticeable because of their façades and profiles, bridges, on the other hand, are frequently overlooked as architectural artifacts. Born of necessity to span streams, valleys, and gorges, bridges are literally underfoot and often inconspicuous. Yet, while sometimes merely utilitarian and unnoticed, many of China's bridges are indeed dramatic, even majestic and daring architectural structures that epitomize the refined use of materials to span space. Joseph Needham, the great scholar of Chinese science and technology, asserted that China's bridges combine "the rational with the romantic," the workaday with the ethereal (1971: 4(3) 145). Unlike a building with walls and a roof wherein the structure is a means to an end, however, the structure of any bridge is as much a means as an end. In addition, a great many traditional Chinese bridges actually had buildings with walls and a roof built atop them, hence the appropriateness of the phrase "architecture over water." Indeed, China's bridges are as much about architecture as they are about engineering in that they combine an inner logic and sense of aesthetics that is distinctive, while giving evidence of a sophisticated empirical approach to construction that equals practices and ingenuity known in the West. Bridge building in China undeniably is much more than a mere footnote in the chronicle of China's contributions to world architecture and engineering.

Bridges sometimes are accidental configurations—a mere log or bamboo thrown over a channel as well as stones deposited by flood across the breadth of a stream—but more often they represent purposeful efforts to tease strength from materials in order to overcome a gap in space. Until recent centuries, bridge building anywhere in the world was a more practical and empirical art than engineering science. Primitive responses using common materials such as wood, stone, and rope of many types progressed over

Right:
Slender logs held together by iron staples and laid across a shallow running stream serve here not only as a temporary bridge but also as a convenient place to wash vegetables. Sanjiang region, Guangxi Zhuang Autonomous Region.

time into more complex solutions using exactly the same materials. Long before science and mathematics were consciously employed to design bridges, local craftsmen experimented with easily accessible materials nearby to solve their bridging needs. Yet, whatever the level of sophistication of the builder or designer, each was forced to consider fundamental and common realities that tested the nature and limits of various forms of matter. In addition, as elsewhere in the world, opportunities emerged in China for exploring and ultimately devising innovative methods of

prevailing over old problems with art and grace using a rich range of technical solutions, many of which actually predated similar advances in the West.

The Basics of Bridges

It will be useful here to spell out some of the basic terms used in later discussions since bridge builders in China, like those anywhere in the world and whatever their sophistication, encountered common forms of matter while searching for, perhaps even stumbling

upon, inspired solutions. Bridges are differentiated in a number of ways, namely in terms of their materials, structure, and purpose.

Traditionally, there were only three types of building materials—resilient wood, durable stone, and flexible ropes—and three types of bridge structures—beam, arch, and suspension. Cement, iron, and steel, among other later materials, came to offer new solutions to contemporary builders even as they continued to work within the traditional range of structural types and tried-and-true old material types. For the most part,

the materials used to build bridges in the past were those that were readily at hand, whether they were timber, stone, or twisted ropes made of bamboo or vines. Yet, as many of the examples shown later in this book reveal, treasured hardwoods, marble, and pliant bamboo somewhat surprisingly came to be used in China in locations far removed from where these materials were commonly found.

The overall configuration of any bridge can be subdivided into its substructure, comprising abutments, piers, and foundations, as well as a super-structure that rises above—beam, arch, suspension, and truss, in addition to any number of combinations of these. Bridge structures differ primarily in the ways in which they bear their own weight, or dead load, as well as the live load—the weight of people, animals, vehicles, even snow. Forces and stresses—tension, compression, torsion, and shear—all impact how successful is the marriage of materials and form in the design and construction of any bridge. In some bridges, these forces act individually, but in most they act in combination, a subject that today is resolved by modeling, but in history was addressed by trial-and-error experimentation.

Tension and compression are opposite forces; the first tends to stretch or elongate something while the second pushes outward. In comparison, torsion is a twisting force, either in one direction while the other end is motionless or twisting in opposite directions. Beside "dead" and "live" loads, the force of the wind, rushing water, and earthquakes can all provide forces that create instability or, in fact, lead to the destruction of any bridge. Arches transfer most of the load they carry diagonally—rather than vertically—to the abutments, pushing outward against these supports rather than transferring their weight downward. In functioning this way, an arch is said to be in a state of compression, with its component parts squeezing outward.

Beams simply rest, with only gravity operating to transfer the weight of the beam and what it carries vertically to the supports on both ends, the abutments, and any midway piers placed to offer supplementary support. Because beams tend to bend at the middle due to downward pull, or tension, perhaps even to the point of breaking, there are definite limits to the length of single beams of different materials. It is sometimes possible to overcome these limits by linking a series of short beams on intervening supporting piers or by projecting the beams by using cantilevering principles. Trusses, which are a form of complex beams, developed in the West in the nineteenth century, were not a solution experimented with by early Chinese bridge builders.

Since stone is very strong in compression, it is naturally the material of choice for building arch bridges. Sometimes called inverted arches, suspension structures are said to be in a state of tension since they pull inward and away from their anchorages. Used in ingenious combinations, beams, arches, and suspended cables can be employed simultaneously to support a bridge. It is all too easy to overbuild, to waste materials, money, and effort.

Elizabeth B. Mock reminds us in her book, *The Architecture of Bridges*, that successful bridge building results from handling "material with poetic insight, revealing its inmost nature while extracting its ultimate strength through structure appropriate to its unique powers" (1949: 7).

In Europe, bridge building languished for eight centuries after the decline of the Roman Empire, not to be revived until the twelfth century. Famed for their extraordinary engineering feats, including bridge building, the Romans left a tangible legacy of stone works that are rivaled by those in China in terms of dates, styles, and geographic spread. Even exceeding in number those still standing in Europe, many examples of early Chinese bridge building innovations can be found throughout the countryside. H. Fugl-Meyer, a twentieth-century Danish engineer, confidently estimated that perhaps 2.5 million bridges existed in China in the 1920s, with as many as fifty-two bridges per square kilometer in some areas of the water-laced Jiangnan region (1937: 33).

Marco Polo himself noted the seeming ubiquity of bridges in Quinsai or Hangzhou, numbering, he said, some 12,000 bridges, an exaggerated figure that might have been inflated by a copyist.

In China, as in other countries, bridges figure not only in legends and myths but are also detailed as part of the material achievements of emperors down through the ages. It is said that the Sage Emperor Yu at the beginning of the third millennium BC summoned giant turtles to position themselves in a river as a means for him to cross. Early bridge builders, recognizing this precursor technique, used a continuous but broken line of large stones to accomplish the same purpose, forming "turtle bridges," a type one can still see in shallow streams throughout the countryside.

As early as the twelfth century BCE, Shang dynasty texts began to employ the contemporary Chinese characters for bridge, *qiao* and *liang*, both of which include the wood radical, explicitly revealing that wood was a common building material for early bridges. Probably simple logs laid side by side rather than hewn timbers were placed across narrow streams or ditches surrounding settlements, as can be seen in the 7000 BP Neolithic Banpo site near contemporary Xi'an. Limited only by the height of available trees, spans were probably lengthened by using "turtle bridges" as piers. Even today in remote mountain areas, it is possible to see somewhat primitive piers built up of stones securely held in cages made of woven bamboo. It is not clear when either wooden or mortared stone piers began to be used to lengthen an effective span.

Step-on Block Bridges

Unlike bridges that span open space in order to allow passage from bank to bank, block stone "bridges" actually take shape through sinking cut stones along a line within a streambed. Their precursor form often was simply a procession of large stones thrown into the water so that a walker could traverse the stream without getting wet. Most step-on stone block bridges or *dingbu*, as they are called in Chinese, comprise a single line of stones, some in their natural form while others have been chiseled into a shape. One of the most elaborate of these stepping-stone links is the 133-meter-long one at Renyang town in the southern part of Taishun county in Zhejiang. With 233 blocks, the passageway has the appearance of piano keys, with one set made of white granite placed higher, while the other lower set is made of darker bluestone. Passersby can step aside so that others may easily go by without slowing their gait, something necessary where heavy loads may be carried on a shoulder pole. Block stone "bridges" are a low-cost response to a critical need for dry passage across a stream. Rarely does floodwater destroy a line of stones of this type, and any movement is relatively easy to repair. Countless others of this type can be seen in the mountains throughout southern China.

Above:
Along this garden path in a back area beyond Du Fu's cottage in Chengdu, Sichuan, these step-on blocks have been molded to appear like lotus leaves.

Left:
Irregularly shaped stones collected from a nearby gorge are set into the streambed in an alternating pattern so that one foot of a pedestrian can easily follow another. Likeng village, Wuyuan county, Jiangxi.

Suspension Bridges

The longest and most sophisticated bridges in the world today are suspension bridges, with a lightness that far surpasses any bridge utilizing beams or arches to span space. China, which is a world leader in the design and construction of modern suspension bridges, has a long and continuing history. Early forms were relatively primitive ropes, hanging as a catenary curve, that were fastened to trees or anchored to stone counterweights on both ends. Pedestrians then could grasp or slide along the cables. In some areas, parallel ropes, held taut at different elevations, made it possible for walkers to tread on one rope while maintaining balance with the other, much like a tentatively supported tightrope walker. Still other suspension bridges involved multiple cables fitted with cradles or baskets into which human beings, animals, or goods could be strapped and then swept across. Over time, suspension bridges evolved to include also a deck covered with wooden cross-planks. It is this last type, with suspended decking and at varying scales, that continues to be seen widely in the dissected mountainous areas of China. While

suspension bridges have an inherent predisposition to sway, undulating in wave-like motions, they nonetheless provide an economical method of linking one side of a valley with the other.

With diminished mass, the grace of a suspension bridge arises from the lines that give it strength—plaited cables fashioned from bamboo, rattan, or other materials of vegetable origin. Marco Polo observed the making of "bamboo rope": "They have canes of the length of fifteen paces, which they split, in their whole length, into very thin pieces, and these, by twisting them together, they form into ropes three hundred paces long. So skillfully are they manufactured, that they are equal in strength to ropes made of hemp."

Although braided metal threads are common in fashioning cables today, iron chains were actually used in China as early as 206 BCE, an innovation that did not appear in Europe until 1741 and in North America until 1796. Among the most notable iron chain suspension bridges is the 113-meter-long Jihong (Rainbow in the Clear Sky) Suspension Bridge in Yunnan, which spans a gorge of the Lancang River and is said to have been crossed by Marco Polo. The bridge seen today was built in 1470. Some suspension bridges, like the Anlan (Tranquil Ripples) Bridge in Sichuan, discussed on pages 156–9, are composed of multiple spans supported by granite in order to overcome the sagging in a span of 300 meters. While cables once were made of braided bamboo, for the past thirty years they have been made of heavy-duty steel wires.

Opposite above and below:
Suspension bridges throughout the mountainous areas of southwestern China are made of thin wire "ropes." The bed of the bridge, which is leveled with rough-hewn timber boards, follows the downward and upward arc of the load-bearing "ropes." Additional "ropes" are used to lift the base "ropes" to prevent excessive sagging and to provide hand-holds for those crossing the swaying span. Anxian, Sichuan.

Above left:
Villagers in mountain areas of Yunnan, as shown here, as well as those in eastern Tibet, traditionally fashioned narrow suspension bridges by fastening ropes made of rattan, a climbing palm with tough stems, to trees on both sides of a gorge.

Above right:
Built in 1629 to span a ravine some 10 meters above the roaring Beipan River in Guizhou, this 50-meter-long suspension bridge was assembled from iron links coupled together into sets of parallel chains. The woodblock print highlights the number of temples and pagodas that populate the area at the rear of the bridge. A statue of Buddha is in the foreground.

Below left:
This unusual *shigandang* (Stone dares to resist evil) totem, with its colorful menacing face, is situated near the head of the suspension bridge to provide protection for the nearby village by preventing harmful influences from crossing the bridge. Anxian, Sichuan.

Below and bottom:
The dozen wrought iron cables and links which constitute the base of this suspension bridge, are anchored into the cement abutments sunken into the earth on both ends of the bridge. Anxian, Sichuan.

Beam Bridges

On the surface, bridges constructed using beams suggest simplicity and lack of distinction, merely wooden or stone planks laid from bank to bank. While many Chinese beam bridges indeed are straightforward and rudimentary, others are surprisingly intricate, even novel. Ordinary beam bridges, supported by intermediate poles and columns as well as crosspieces, are features commonly present in the pastoral scenes of Chinese paintings, reflecting perhaps their ease of construction and ubiquity in the countryside. Substantial beam bridges made of timbers and supported by stone piers are among the earliest bridge type described in Chinese historical chronicles, with a history that reaches at least to the second millennium BCE.

Qinshihuang, the first emperor of Qin who unified China in 221 BCE and is noted for his construction of walls and roads, also built notable beam bridges. During his reign, an imposing, multiple-span bridge—18 meters wide and some 544 meters long—was built near the Qin capital at Xianyang. Eight-meter-long timber planks were used to form each of the sixty-eight spans that rested on massive cut-stone columns sunk into the bottom of the Wei He River. During the Han dynasty that followed the Qin, at least two more large beam-type bridges and numerous smaller ones were built in the region around the

Above:
This rubbing from a carved brick from the Eastern Han period (CE 25–220) shows a horse-drawn carriage passing over a stone and slab wood bridge.

Below:
Just outside the imposing gate of the walled city, as depicted in Zhang Zeduan's twelfth-century painting, *Qingming shanghe tu*, is a moat crossed by a broad

bridge. Probably made of stone and wood beams, it clearly had sufficient strength and width to accommodate throngs of animals, humans, and carts. © Palace Museum, Beijing.

山鷹奇觀
清呵渚騎有閒在山淨源通二月餘後見甘棠過
湖府忽看浮を艶圖書鏡鋪洪湖を波泥靡
托珍蘢玉浪客好特桃花委辰凌農辰弹翅起化

Above:
Shrouded in a misty atmosphere, this landscape painting titled *Waters Rise in Spring* by Shitao (1642–1707) features a common beam bridge using a trestle-like structure of slim poles and crosspieces. © Shanghai Museum.

Right and far right:
Constructed of modular sets of supporting legs, crosspieces, and wooden planks, long trestle bridges of this type are common in the villages of southern Anhui and northern Jiangxi.

flourishing imperial capital of Chang'an, just to the south of Xianyang. Several of these continued in use until the Tang dynasty, serving as important conduits along the fabled Silk Road. Piers of timber, stone, and iron as well as cylinders formed from bamboo containing rocks and earth, some dug into the muddy river bottom, supported bridges of this type. In a Han-dynasty tomb chamber, which was opened in today's Inner Mongolia in 1971, a painted image of striking proportions of a wooden beam bridge crossing the Wei He River was revealed. Using rather slim stone columns and wooden beams, this bridge represents a type found widely in many areas of northern and northwestern China.

Not all wooden beam bridges spanned streams. Indeed, some snaked their way as timber trestle structures through inhospitable topography using building practices that improved upon those employed in shorter wooden beam bridges. Unrivalled in the world is the elevated timber plank bridge-road system that linked the cradle of Chinese civilization in the Wei He River valley of Shaanxi province in the northwest with the fertile Sichuan Basin in the southwest. Well known in Chinese history as the Shudao or "Road to Sichuan" and built at least as early as the Han period (206 BCE– CE 220), the wooden plank trestle bridge served as a channel of administrative, military, and cultural communication as well as trade for some 2,000 years across the formidable barrier of the Qinling and Daba ranges. Although the road fell into decay in the nineteenth

century, portions of it are still used by local mountain dwellers to pass from one watershed to another and to avoid swiftly moving streams in narrow river gorges.

About a third of the 700-kilometer-long Linking Cloud Road, which forms a significant portion of the Shudao as it threads its way through the rugged Qinling Range, is actually comprised of wooden trestle shelves built out from canyon sides or astride streambeds. Termed *gedao* and *zhandao*, literally "hanging" bridges, timber plankways involved sinking wooden substructures into nearly vertical cliffs in order to support the plank paths. Herold J. Wiens, a geographer who studied the Shudao, explains that repairs and reconstruction taking three years during the Later Han period (CE 25–220) required the conscripted labor of 766,800 men working some 23 million man-days. During the Tang dynasty (618–907), the celebrated Buddhist monk Xuan Zang, accompanied by the Monkey King, wrote of *zhandao* as well as rope bridges, iron chains, and wooden ladders necessary to traverse the dangerous precipices of the region on his pilgrimage west. Structurally daring and indeed sometimes dangerous, trestle frameworks—with horizontal, vertical, and slanted supports—have even been employed in the building of imaginative temple structures on the sides of high precipices, such as the celebrated Hanging Temple at Datong in northern Shanxi province.

Stone beam bridges—most short but many comprising multiple spans—eventually became the most

Above:
Timber plank trestle bridges called *zhandao* have long been common in western Sichuan. Their construction involves sinking wooden substructures into nearly vertical cliffs in order to support the plank paths laid on them.

Right:
The sprawling painting titled *Emperor Minghuang's Journey to Shichuan*, a Ming copy after an original by Qiu Ying (1494–1552), details the flight of Emperor Xuanzong and the imperial concubine Yang Guifei from Chang'an, today's Xi'an, southward along the Shudao or "Road to Sichuan" in order to escape the An Lushan Rebellion of 755.
© Freer Gallery of Art, Smithsonian Institution, Washington, DC.

common and permanent bridge form in southern China. Resting atop piers of piled carved stone placed parallel to the flow of the stream, many stone beam bridges are quite simple, while many also are quite complex in that they are supported by massive pier structures built up within midstream cofferdams. Even a cursory examination reveals that stone beam bridges require more substantial abutments and piers than bridges built using timbers. Cantilevering the beams, as discussed below, made it possible to extend the span. The engineer Fugl-Meyer critiqued building in stone with his observation that "the Chinese bridge builder taxes his material to the utmost without

allowing for any margin of safety. When a stone has a hidden fault ... or when it is overloaded, it collapses without causing any surprise, and is replaced by a new stone of the same dimensions" (1937: 59–60). Metamorphosed granite, which varies in hues of gray and is rather coarse in texture, is the most widely used material for stone beam bridges.

Perhaps the longest multiple-span stone beam bridge—one extant single segment has 150 spans with a total length of some 390 meters—is actually the remnant of a 1–2 kilometer-long towpath, called *qiandao* in Chinese. Overall, there are some 7.5 kilometers of stone paths still standing, a fraction of

stone pathway, but in others the towpath was very much like a bridge as stone beams supported by stone piers rose a meter or so above the water. In terms of materials used and techniques of construction, towpaths differed little from common stone beam bridges that crossed streams. Each of the piers supporting the towpath is composed of a stack of granite blocks approximately 1.5 meters thick. Each span between them is made up of three or more rough-cut stone beams that exceed 2 meters in length and have a width of 3 meters. At intervals along the towpath, a section is elevated to permit the passage of small boats plying the intricate canal network of this region.

An outstanding and complex stone beam bridge with many components is the Bazi (Character Eight) Bridge in the southeastern section of Shaoxing, Zhejiang, a city that had in 1903 some 229 fine bridges along its 29 canals. The oldest extant urban bridge in China, the Bazi was constructed in 1256 during the later Song dynasty. Located to meet the needs of foot and water traffic at the junction of three canals and three lanes, the structure is actually made up of two juxtaposed bridges that are reminiscent of the Chinese character ba 八 representing the number eight. The

what once existed. These towpaths were constructed between 1862 and 1874 along the Xiaoshan-Shaoxing Canal in Zhejiang province to extend canal transport beyond the terminus of the Grand Canal at Hangzhou eastward to the seaport at Ningbo. The towpath thus served as a passageway for trackers who were needed to pull the heavily laden boats along. While the canal boats were usually propelled by sails or by sculling, sometimes it was necessary to tow them when strong seasonal winds made sailing difficult.

Some portions of the towpath were built immediately adjacent to land; indeed, at some locations trackers actually moved on land before reaching another

Opposite above:
This view is from atop the Bazi (Character Eight) Bridge, today covered in vines, towards a canalside neighborhood of low-rise dwellings that retains much of its traditional life.

Opposite below:
Rather complex in terms of its scale and ingenious construction, the Bazi Bridge nonetheless is essentially a bridge constructed of long beams and smaller blocks of granite in carefully assembled stacks.

Top:
The gradual incline of a set of steps makes it possible for two adjacent canals to be connected.

Above:
As this model clearly reveals, the Bazi Bridge is actually a combination of two bridges juxtaposed so that it connects multiple lanes while facilitating canal traffic.

principal span clears 4.5 meters, rises some 5 meters, and has a width of 3.2 meters. Four-meter-long stone columns are slightly cambered to support the main span. The columns are themselves supported by a double layer of quarried stone 1.8 meters thick atop a foundation of stone boulders, which together constitute the support for the abutments. Including the balustrades and approach steps, the bridge is assembled from countless quarried slabs forming a structure of incalculable weight and substantial versatility that fits compactly into a tight residential environment. Overall the stepped approaches are gentle and have been modified to facilitate the movement of carts and bicycles.

Handling large timbers and heavy stone columns set limits to what bridge builders could accomplish with available materials. In the middle two centuries of the Song dynasty (960–1279), extraordinary megalithic stone bridges built with granite piers and granite beams began to be built along the embayed shoreline of Fujian in southeastern China. The broad tidal inlets at the mouths of short turbulent rivers provided substantial challenges to spanning them with structures of any type, let alone utilizing megaliths. The methods employed in building massive stone bridges in Fujian remain a relative mystery, but there is no doubt that more than ordinary skills were required to maneuver

Above:
With the tide in, the mudflats beneath the Luoyang Bridge in Quanzhou are submerged. The prow-like triangular cutwaters point upstream.

Left:
This is a remnant of a long nineteenth-century stone beam towpath along the Xiaoshan-Shaoxing Canal that extended water transport beyond the Hangzhou terminus of the Grand Canal. When there was little wind to fill the sails of boats, trackers on the towpaths used ropes to pull the heavily laden boats.

stone slabs that reached 20 meters in length and 200 metric tons in weight. It is an amazing feat that stone beam bridges totaling 15 kilometers in length were constructed in a relatively brief thirty-year period alone throughout Fujian to help integrate an expanding transportation network. While there may once have been a bridge nearly three times longer, the Anping (Peace) Bridge, built between 1138 and 1151, is today heralded as "no bridge under the sun is as long as this one." The bridge, which today is 2070 meters long, 10 percent shorter than it once was, was constructed using 6–7 granite slabs, each of which is 8–10 meters long, laid atop 331 stone piers. Another remarkable megalithic bridge still standing is the Luoyang Bridge, begun about 1053 and completed in six years. Today, only some 800 meters of the bridge's original 1100-meter length and 31 of 47 piers remain. Some of the 11-meter-long granite slabs forming the deck weigh as much as 150 metric tons and were positioned using the ebb and flow of the tides. Bridge builders utilized an ingenious method of securing components of the stone foundations by employing living oysters as an organic mastic within crevices in the stone in order to strengthen the structure.

Floating Bridges

King Wen, who laid the foundation for the Zhou dynasty some 3,000 years ago, is said to have made one of the earliest technological improvements over simple wooden beam bridges by lashing together boats to form a floating or pontoon bridge across the Wei He River. Employing side-by-side boats that then held up wooden planks, essentially beams laid transversely across the boats, floating bridges of this type became quite common in China as a means to span wide and deep, even swiftly moving streams. In general, pontoon bridges cope well with fluctuations in water level, variations in stream velocity, and the common need to accommodate navigation by other boats. At relatively low cost, pontoon bridges provided a relatively quick solution to a need in facilitating land transport. While small boats provide the support for most floating bridges, in China bamboo rafts, barrels, animal skins, wagon wheels, even calabashes have been used to support logs and planks. Pontoon bridges are usually formed a section at a time until the opposite bank is reached. In addition to cables and chains linking the boats together, "stones turtles"—woven containers of stone rubble—were sometimes dropped to the stream's floor as anchors to moor groups of boats. Floating bridges demanded careful monitoring in response to river flow and traffic so that cables and anchorages could be adjusted to keep approaches relatively level.

In many parts of the world, floating bridges are viewed only as temporary structures, but in China many have endured for centuries. In one fashion or another, floating bridges made of linked wooden boats have stretched across the Gan River in Ganzhou, Jiangxi, since the Song dynasty. However, today only the Dongjin Bridge, with a length of 400 meters across 100 small wooden boats, remains. While most floating bridges provided only a mere walkway for pedestrians or simple wheeled carts, others in the twentieth century were capable of bearing vehicular traffic such as cars, trucks, and buses across two lanes. During warfare especially, pontoons were capable of being assembled quickly, serving a purpose, and then removed before they could be used by one's enemies.

China's most important rivers, the Huang He or Yellow River and the Chang Jiang or Yangzi River, both have several millennia-long histories of being spanned by precursor pontoon bridges, even as constructed bridges did not span them until the middle of the twentieth century. The Huang He saw its first floating bridge in 541 BCE and the Chang Jiang in CE 35, with dozens more built in the centuries following that utilized improvements in anchorages and connections. In Yongji county in southern

Shanxi, the restoration of the Puji Floating Bridge during the Tang dynasty in 724 brought with it an especially noteworthy innovation—the use of heavy cast iron anchorages in the shape of large recumbent oxen that were secured with other weighty shoreline anchorages by a series of iron chains that replaced bamboo cables. Excavated only in 1989, these iron oxen were approximately 3.3 meters long, 1.5 meters high, and about 15 tons in weight, and were joined as well by life-size iron figures of men.

In some ways, pontoon bridges are reminiscent of what takes shape in a Chinese tale of love regarding the Milky Way, which Chinese traditionally saw as a luminous "silver stream" in the heavens. On the seventh day of the seventh month each year, Niu Lang and Zhi Nu, a cowherd and a weaving girl, were allowed to meet when all the magpies on earth flew to heaven and formed a bridge over the galactic stream for them to cross and meet.

Right:
Although rarely photographed, pontoon bridges of this type were created utilizing bamboo poles lashed together and then floated on the water. To ease passage on foot, a long mat made of thin slats of woven bamboo was laid across the floating slender bamboo poles.

Below:
In this photograph taken in the 1930s somewhere in southern China, there is only one gap in the adjacent boats that can be opened for river traffic to pass through.

Cantilevered Beam Bridges

Simple wooden and stone beams have limits to the distances they can span, rarely reaching 10 meters. Each quarried stone or cut timber, the most common materials traditionally employed in cantilevered bridges, has an unspecified strength depending on the species and type. Even when they appear homogeneous, each usually contains invisible pockets of weakness. Downward pressures brought on by an increased live load can lead to unanticipated structural failure, the rapid breaking of the beam as it exceeds its ability to bend. It is not surprising then, that practical experience led to the doubling or tripling of beams in order to increase strength, and a sequenced layering in order to extend the range.

Chinese bridge builders began in the fourth century CE to employ the cantilever principle—the layering of counterbalanced beams with each set of segments supporting additional beams that reach out towards a midpoint—in order to extend the clear span. This approach involved projecting out horizontal arms of wood, then later stone beams from weighted abutments of piled stone or masonry. Since a gap usually still remained, this opening between them was then spanned with a beam or set of beams. Single-span cantilevered wooden bridges, usually using logs, were frequently built to cross relatively narrow ravines in Yunnan and Sichuan provinces as well as in remote areas of Tibet. In Gansu, even relatively shallow streams were bridged by structures that soared using a cantilevered superstructure.

Above:
At the Chengyang Bridge in Ma'an village, Sanjiang, Guangxi, layers of protruding logs separated by transverse timbers provide cantilevered lifting for the covered bridge.

Multiple spans of this type, each comprised of pairs of cantilevered supports, are found today in central and eastern China, especially in Fujian, Guangxi, Hunan, and Zhejiang provinces.

Among the most notable cantilevered wooden bridges in China are the "wind-and-rain" bridges or *fengyu qiao* of the Dong minority group in southern China. Although the most notable feature of *fengyu qiao* is the series of colorful pavilions lined along their continuous galleried superstructure, the support beneath is also outstanding since it is usually comprised of sets of massive cantilevered logs. The Chengyang Bridge is another good example. With a length of 77.76 meters and four 17.3-meter-wide openings set upon five piers, it was constructed between 1912 and 1924 in the Sanjiang region of the Guangxi Zhuang Autonomous Region. Three cantilevered layers of fir logs—a series of projecting horizontal beams 7–8 meters in length—are laid longitudinally across the top of each of the five stone piers. Between the four levels of cantilevered logs, which are held firm by tenoned timbers, are thin spacer logs that together stabilize the support and also provide some degree of flexibility. In this region, as elsewhere in southern China, when rebuilding of dilapidated cantilevered structures took place, the length of spans could be maintained by cantilevering more logs of shorter length than were originally used. The Lujiang Bridge in Hunan province, first built in the middle of the thirteenth century and rebuilt many times, at one point had ten layers of cantilevered logs to enable its span.

Arch Bridges

Arches in many shapes and configurations, employing both stone and wood as materials, epitomize the superlative achievements of Chinese bridge building. Stone arch bridges are ubiquitous in China, but arches constructed of timbers, which are sometimes called "rainbow bridges," are much more limited in their extent. Varying widely in form and in clear span, many arch bridges are merely functional and rather primitive, while others display not only astonishing design skills and techniques of construction but also express exquisite beauty. It is not known definitively when the first stone or timber arch bridges emerged in China but both

forms developed independently of those in the West. Since arches are stronger than planks, whether the material is stone or wood, the evolution of arch forms made for the possibility of greater spans and heights. Arches are said to be in compression, pushing outward rather than transferring their weight downward as with planks, and as a result require substantial foundations.

Above left:
Activities along as well as in the water beneath an arch bridge crossing the Si River in Shandong province, are exhibited in this rubbing from an engraved brick of the Eastern Han period (CE 25–220).

Left:
Carved on the surface of a baked brick, this image depicts a horse-drawn carriage and a porter with a carrying pole crossing an arch bridge, which is reinforced with vertical supports beneath.

Below left:
This tableaux of county scenes in Huizhou, found today in a temple near the Bei'an Bridge in southern Anhui province, includes a steep single-arch bridge with a pavilion atop it.

Right:
Although the scholars drinking in the wooded countryside are the main theme of Shitao's early eighteenth-century *Drunk in Autumn Woods*, this virtuosic painting incorporates elements that could be found in a small park or garden, including a fine bridge, pavilions, and paths. © The Metropolitan Museum of Art, New York.

Below:
Shown in this painting by a European is a somewhat fanciful bridge with billowing ornamentation above it that was clearly built so that large vessels, shown in the foreground, could pass easily beneath its soaring arch.

Stone Arch Bridges

In southern China, single- and multiple-arch bridges often rise precipitously above narrow canals, while others lay close to the water, with a continuous pattern of repeating arches from bank to bank, a form that is also common in northern China. Among the earliest representations of stone arch bridges are those of the Eastern Han period (CE 25–220) inscribed on fired brick tiles that have been excavated from underground tombs—themselves often constructed with arch ceilings—throughout northern China. In Henan province, a brick reveals an unadorned curved span being crossed by pedestrians, a mounted horse, and a carriage drawn by four horses with boats and fish beneath. The steep approaches are apparent, reinforced by the presence of muscular men towing the carriage up the deck, with others controlling the carriage as it descends.

The arch is a shape that carries its load outward as a result of compression that produces horizontal outward thrusts towards the bridge's abutments. In spite of the durability of stone, moreover, Chinese stone arch bridges reveal a remarkable plasticity, a "resisting by yielding," according to Chinese bridge builders. Throughout the Jiangnan region, where sandy soil made it difficult to sink solid foundations, bridge builders learned to make use of vertical sheer walls of stone slabs to receive those forces that might tend to deform the arch. The Chinese rarely used mortar as a bond between stones. Rather, stones were generally carefully shaped and sometimes mortised

Above:
One of China's most beautiful arch bridges is the Taiping (Heavenly Peace) Bridge along the canal between Hangzhou and Ningbo to the west of the city of Shaoxing, Zhejiang. Built first in 1620 and then again in 1858, it is well known for its exquisite carved balustrades.

Left:
The lofty Wumen (Wu Gate) Bridge in Suzhou, Jiangsu, is located along the Grand Canal near the important Pan Gate. Said to date to the Song dynasty, it was rebuilt in the middle of the nineteenth century to a length of 63 meters.

Above:
In the countryside of southern Huizhou, straddling the border between today's Anhui and Jiangxi provinces, countless old stone arch bridges still serve today's villagers. Although this bridge has a name, Qingjin (Celebrate Gold) Bridge, no information is available on its history.

Left:
A small unnamed single-arch bridge along the canal east of Shaoxing, Zhejiang.

into each other or joined together by overlapping iron cramps. As a result of these techniques and the ensuing elasticity of the stone shell, stone arch bridges could tolerate a high degree of deformation without the bridge collapsing.

Chinese stonecutters clearly accumulated experience that led logically to the development of different styles of bridges. Relatively crude semicircular single-arch spans can be seen in many areas of southern China, some of which are quite old. Many, however, are of more recent origin, the handiwork of local artisans who gather stones from nearby streambeds in order to fashion serviceable workaday bridges as others did for centuries before them. Semicircular arches of dressed stone dot the Chinese landscape in large numbers. Descriptive names such as "horse's hoof," "egg-shaped," "pot bottom," and "pointed" are suggestive of other variations of

elliptical and parabolic shapes. Some arches are polygons comprised of interlocked rectangular stone beams. Arches of this type echo similar ones found in Chinese tombs as well as gates through city walls, and even the Great Wall. While permitting a greater span than simple beams, polygonal beam bridges are, however, structurally weaker than true arch bridges. On the other hand, as the number of inclined stone beam segments in a multisided polygonal bridge increases from three to as many as seven, the structure begins to function much like a true arch bridge.

Many stone arch bridges are infilled with earth and have seams between the cut stone that tends to allow dust to accumulate, filling the spaces so that, in time, seeds are able to germinate. As the roots of plants grow, they then have the capacity of loosening the stone blocks, shifting them sometimes to a point where gravity brings portions of the bridge down. It is not uncommon, even today, as can be seen in many photographs, for plants of all sorts to grow out from a bridge. In colder areas, moreover, these conditions are compounded because of the freezing and thawing of water that runs into or builds up in the seams, again with the means of dislodging the stone and leading to failure of the structure.

Segmental Arch Stone Bridges

Among the most remarkable achievements of Chinese bridge building—indeed an advancement unrivalled in the world—was the creation of a segmental arch bridge at the end of the sixth century and beginning of the seventh century. This innovation, which predated similar forms in the West by 800 years—repudiated the convention that a semicircular arch was necessary to transfer the weight of a bridge downwards to where the arch tangentially meets the pier. The celebrated Zhaozhou Bridge, China's oldest standing bridge and the oldest open spandrel bridge in the world, seemingly flies forth from its abutments. The double pair of openings piercing both ends of the arch spandrel, which at once accentuate its lithe curvature, lighten the weight of the bridge and

Left:
When this photograph was taken sometime before 1928, the Zhaozhou Bridge had been altered somewhat and there was sufficient water in the stream for vessels with sails to pass.

facilitate the diversion of flood waters by allowing them to pass through the auxiliary arches rather than pound against the spandrels.

Following the pattern of the Zhaozhou, also called Anji (Safe Passage) and Dashi (Great Stone), Bridge, no fewer than four were built in nearby areas of Hebei province where natural conditions were similar, while at least twenty others were constructed in northern China as well as in Guizhou and Guangxi. Until the middle of the twentieth century, the Zhaozhou Bridge was the longest single-arch span bridge in China. The restoration of the Zhaozhou to its original form and the building of similar bridges in recent times confirm that the Chinese recognize their early achievements in engineering technique and aesthetic expression. A masterpiece built almost 1,400 years ago, the Zhaozhou Bridge foreshadowed the elegance and scale of many contemporary bridges. In terms of economy of materials and aesthetic qualities, it is clearly the direct ancestor of the relatively light and lithe modern reinforced concrete bridges that dispense with stonework between the curvature of the arch and the flat deck above. As discussed on pages 123–7, the circumstances surrounding the construction of the Zhaozhou Bridge reveal the conscious attention to natural conditions, transportation requirements, and available materials, in addition to inspired creativity.

Top:
Although built more than 1,400 years ago, the Zhaozhou Bridge in Hebei appears like a contemporary bridge because of its low line and open spandrels.

Above:
As with the Zhaozhou Bridge, each of the double sets of openings that pierce the arch spandrel on both ends of the smaller Yongtong (Eternal Crossing) Bridge reduces the weight of the structure and eases the flow-through of water during flood.

Multiple Arch Bridges

Multiple arch bridges are widely found in China, compelling evidence of both the diffusion of designs throughout the empire and the innovative skills of local bridge builders. Surprisingly monumental structures in what are today backward villages stand as a testament to the vitality of road and river transport in centuries past, the same commercial energy that gave rise to the magnificent mansions of merchants and gentry in out-of-the-way places. As with multiple-span beam bridges, arches were linked together to bridge greater distances than was possible with a single arch. Almost always an odd number, ranging from as few as three to as many as seventy, the duplication of spans almost always invokes pleasing rhythm with its repeating elements. Arch bridges with three spans are especially common in Jiangsu and Zhejiang provinces in a region of a dense canal network. Soft alluvial soils in this low-lying region meant that bridges had to be relatively light. In addition, it was necessary for the bridges to rise rather high so as not to obstruct the passage of canal boats, many of which were powered by sails attached to tall masts. Unlike in the north, land transport of goods rarely involved carts or animals but depended upon individuals carrying shoulder poles who were capable of mounting steps as long as they could maintain their gait. Today, cyclists must dismount as they approach a steep bridge, but it is not difficult to push even a loaded bicycle up one of the ramps that have been added to the steps in recent times. Triple-arch bridges typically have a large central span, approximately 20 percent longer than the pair of identical smaller side arches. The two piers of such bridges are usually relatively thin given the spans they support, the load of adjacent arches being carried by the shared piers. Even though some triple-span bridges appear frail, insufficiently massive to carry the load of the arch shell, balustrades, and walkway, they are capable of substantial loads. Although only a small number of five-, seven-, and nine-span stone arch bridges survive, they differ little in structure from more modest three-span bridges, with loads being passed from one arch ring to another until reaching the abutments.

Records indicate that the longest multi-span thin-pier stone arch bridge, which crossed an arm of Taihu Lake just outside the city wall of Wujiang in Jiangsu province, was constructed in 1325 during the Yuan dynasty to replace a shorter wooden span on stone piers that had been built in 1066 and subsequently modified several times. Although called the Chuihong (Hanging Rainbow) Bridge, the structure did not soar. Instead, it was built only slightly elevated above the water except for several triple-arch segments that rose to facilitate the passage of vessels beneath. Until 1967 and the collapse of many sections, it stood as China's longest multiple arch bridge at 450 meters with 72 spans. Only 49.3 meters and ten arches remain on the east end of the original bridge, today protected within a park. Restoration efforts continue to dredge up fallen

Top:
The 140-meter-long Ziyang (Purple Sun) Bridge in Shexian county, Anhui, is said to have been built during the reign of Wanli (1572–1620) in the Ming dynasty, but the bridge seen today was completed in 1835. Given its length and width, the bridge is a remarkably light structure, with eight stone piers and nine arches.

Above:
The Renji (Benevolent Aid) Bridge, completed during the Ming dynasty and rebuilt after a flood in 1868 with contributions from local folk, is 79 meters long and supported by four stone piers. With the equally old Pingzheng (Peaceful Governance) Bridge in the background, the pair is considered a place for townspeople to welcome the new moon. Qimen county, Anhui.

Right:
Close-up of the bow-shaped cutwaters of the 89-meter-long Pingzheng Bridge in Qimen county, Anhui. Records show the construction of bridges at this site during both the Song and Ming dynasties. After being destroyed in a disastrous flood in 1830, it was not until the nineteenth century that it was rebuilt. In 1974, the bridge was strengthened and widened.

arches, which then are added to the original span. Few Chinese bridges have received the accolades from poets and painters as has the Chuihong Bridge.

No currently standing multiple arch bridge is longer than the Baodai (Precious Belt) Bridge, which spans 317 meters, with fifty low arches and three mid-span higher arches that permit boat traffic. As a low-lying bridge with thin stone piers, its appearance is said to resemble the jade belt donated by the governor who financed its construction. Built first in the early ninth century during the Tang dynasty, it took its current form about 1446 in the Ming dynasty. Adjacent to a broad section of the Grand Canal some 7 kilometers southeast of Suzhou, the replicated arches of the Baodai Bridge span the Dantai River as it empties into the Grand Canal. It was constructed as a link in a towpath which otherwise would have been broken

Above:
Built first in the early ninth century, the Baodai (Precious Belt) Bridge is actually an elegant towpath extending 317 meters along the Grand Canal, which took its current form during the Ming dynasty. In addition to lengthy abutments that jut out from the shore, fifty-three arches cross open water for 250 meters.

Far left:
Squeezed between modern structures, this triple-arch span is just one of many remarkable bridges in Jinze, a watertown now swallowed up in the suburbs of Shanghai.

Left:
Accompanying a vocalist, the performer plays a traditional *erhu*, a long-necked instrument, near the five-arch Fangsheng (Liberating Living Things) Bridge in Zhujiajiao watertown in the suburbs of Shanghai.

because of the confluence of the two water bodies. The bridge was rebuilt in 1872 after a major collapse during the Taiping Rebellion, a subject discussed on pages 198–9, and restored in 1956. Once regularly visited to enjoy its technical achievements, today few seek out the bridge because of its remoteness, except during the Mid-Autumn Festival when the stone pavement affords a commodious space to view the full moon.

In northern China, the celebrated Lugou (Reed Gulch) Bridge has similar renown to that of the Baodai Bridge in the Jiangnan region. Built between 1189 and 1192 during the Jin dynasty, the bridge, with a span of 266.5 meters, was visited in 1280 by Marco Polo, who described it as "perhaps unequaled by any other in the world." Building the bridge presented distinct challenges due to the fact that the often shallow Yongding River, which it crossed, usually iced over during cold winters in its upper reaches, and then in early spring disgorged ice floes made up of enormous blocks. To counter this, massive stone piers as well as boat-shaped cutwaters on the upstream side of each pier were positioned to deflect or break up the ice as it passed through the eleven arches.

Like other northern bridges, the Lugou's deck is quite flat to facilitate the passage of carts pulled by human beings, mules, donkeys, horses, and camels. The 485 small stone lions that sit atop the capitals along the balustrades on both sides of the Lugou Bridge are one of its special characteristics.

Timber Arch Rainbow Bridges

Rainbow bridges—ingenious arches using "woven" timbers as the underlying structure—until recently were believed to have been lost in the twelfth century. The image preserved in Zhang Zeduan's twelfth-century Song painting *Qingming shanghe tu*, usually translated as "Going Up the River During the Qingming Festival," portrays an interlocked arch of piled beams that allowed large vessels to pass beneath its humpbacked 18.5-meter-long arch. With a width of 9.4 meters, the bridge provided ample space for one of the bustling markets of Kaifeng, the Song imperial capital. In recent decades, reports emerged of bridges with a similar structure—but with the addition of covered corridors—in the remote mountains of Fujian and Zhejiang provinces.

It is noteworthy that more than a hundred variations of covered rainbow bridges have been recently "discovered." But it is a strange fact that no *uncovered* bridge with an underlying timber frame, like that shown in Zhang Zeduan's scroll, has ever been located and documented.

Local people refer to the bridges that seem to rear up abruptly from their abutments and then soar dramatically cross steep chasms as "centipede bridges" because of their resemblance to the arch-like rise of a long arthropod's body as it crawls. From a distance, these bridges appear to be supported by a type of wooden arch, but in actual fact it is an illusionary "arch" that emerges from the interlinking of a series of logs—long tree trunks—that function as interwoven chords or segments of the "arch." Chinese engineers refer to such a structure as a "woven timber arch," "combined beam timber arch," and "woven timber

arch-beam" to underscore the use of straight timber members tied together. The basic components are quite simple: two pairs of two layered sets of inclined timbers, with one set embedded in opposite abutments, stretch upward toward the middle of the stream. To fill the gap between these inclined timber sets, two horizontally trending assemblages of timbers are attached. Transverse timbers tenoned to them and/or tied with rattan or rope hold each of the sets of timbers together. It is these warp and weft elements that give rise to the term "woven."

The downward pressure of the heavy logs compresses all the components together into a tight and relatively stable composition with a significant bearing

Bottom:
No "rainbow bridge" is more famous than the one depicted in Zhang Zeduan's twelfth-century celebrated *Qingming shanghe tu* scroll, a section of which portrays an interlocked arch of piled beams permitting even large vessels to pass beneath its humpbacked opening. Along the surface of the bridge as well as in nearby lanes are busy markets. © Palace Museum, Beijing.

capacity, the equilibrium can be upset if forces from beneath—such as might come from torrential floods or typhoon winds—push upward. To further stabilize the underlying structure, additional weight is added by constructing an often elaborate building atop the bridge. Somewhat counter intuitively, the heavy timber columns, beams, balustrades, and roof tiles add a substantial dead load that actually increases stability. With the addition of wooden skirts along the side perimeter, the wooden members are then also protected from weathering and deterioration to create a covered bridge. In the West, the covering of a covered bridge is *always* described as being added in order to protect the underlying wooden structure from weather, and *never* as added weight to stabilize the structure.

In 1999, an American television crew associated with the science series NOVA worked with a team of Chinese scholars and timber craftsmen to design and build a Chinese bridge. Believed at the time to be attempting something unknown except in a twelfth-century painting, the project successfully completed a model bridge that still stands in Jinze, a canal town on the shores of Dianshang Lake in the western suburbs of Shanghai. Working without plans and increasingly aware of how difficult the tasks were, the team experimented with materials and techniques to create an interlaced superstructure of beams placed under and over girders that metamorphosed from a beam to an arch structure. Their bridge is a modest one when compared with those still found in southern Zhejiang and northern Fujian or even the one depicted by Zhang Zeduan.

Far surpassing this modest effort to create a rainbow bridge reminiscent of the one in Kaifeng

are the numerous covered bridges with similar structures in Zhejiang and Fujian provinces, details of which are given on pages 218–47. A fine example, not discussed there, is Xianju (Home of the Immortals) Bridge, about 20 kilometers from the Taishun county town. Built first in 1452 and then rebuilt in 1673, it has the longest span of any bridge of this type in Taishun—34.14 meters—and an overall length of 41.83 meters. The bridge was spared when the highway was improved with an adjacent modern bridge. Rising like a slithering centipede, the covered gallery of the Xianju Bridge utilizes eighty slender pillars to fashion its nineteen internal bays. The rooftop ornamentation is especially notable.

Opposite above:
In 1999, in Jinze, a watertown suburb of Shanghai, a modest "rainbow bridge" was built as part of the NOVA television series to re-create the wooden substructure of the famed twelfth-century *Qingming shanghe tu* using "woven" timbers to form an arch-like interlocking structure.

Below:
Rising high enough for motorized vessels to move beneath it, Jinze's newly constructed timber "rainbow bridge" joins many very old stone bridges along the nearby canals.

Covered Bridges

Many of the covered bridges in China are not rainbow bridges because they have underlying supports that differ from the woven timber arch-beam structure. The genesis of covered bridges in China, with traditions that predate covered bridges elsewhere in the world, is quite varied and the forms that are still seen are strikingly different from those that occur in Europe and North America. Covered bridges emerged in Europe in the fourteenth century, principally in mountainous areas in Bulgaria and Switzerland, before subsequently being built throughout the continent. While the few covered bridges remaining today in Europe are individually distinct and historically important, they generally do not have the aura of romance and nostalgia that wafts about covered bridges in North America. In the United States and Canada, covered bridges became common only in the first decade of the nineteenth century, subsequently becoming iconic elements of American rural and urban landscapes when horse-drawn vehicles dominated. Using patented truss designs, they proliferated until 1855 when the introduction of improved steel alternatives led to a dramatic drop off in their construction. Over the years, fire, flooding, vandalism, rotting, and overloaded vehicles swept away thousands of wooden covered bridges. Today, fewer than a thousand covered bridges remain of the 14,000 once standing in North America, where wooden covered bridges are universally recognized as worthy of preservation and valued as emblems of times past. Today, it is estimated that at least 3,000 covered bridges are in existence in China, a number that far exceeds those elsewhere in the world, and are among the oldest structures still standing. Yet, old bridges continue to be lost due to floods, typhoons, vandalism, fire, and replacement by modern bridges to meet current needs. It is often difficult to spot the ruins of old covered bridges because timbers and stone are usually quickly scavenged for use as building materials elsewhere.

While old photographs of bridges in China frequently pointed to the existence of small structures atop even single-arch stone bridges or to pavilions along longer bridges, rarely were large ostentatious structures photographed, probably because they were not encountered. Indeed, until very recently long covered bridges in China were essentially unknown outside China. Yet, whether the covered housing sits atop several stone columns, a series of brick or stone arches, a cantilevered wooden structure, or a "woven timber arch-beam," it is now apparent that the Chinese constructed some of the most complex, most ornamented, and most beautiful covered bridges in the world. The renovation, rebuilding, and new construction of covered bridges in China have been increasing in recent decades. While many of these various types will be extensively discussed on pages 218–61, some will be introduced here.

Most covered bridges in China are constructed in exactly the same fashion as local houses and temples, using timber frame construction and a conventional set of elementary parts. The superstructure of the bridge serves as the "foundation," with the floor of the bridge being paved with bricks or stone or overlain with sawn timber. Most covered bridges are I-shaped structures that are comprised of the number of bays necessary to span a particular distance. Often, as with land-based structures, the number of bays is an odd number since such numbers are considered auspicious. Wooden benches, some quite elaborately made, usually run along the full length of any covered bridge. Some of these covered bridges are analogous to roadside pavilions, differing only in that they span a body of water.

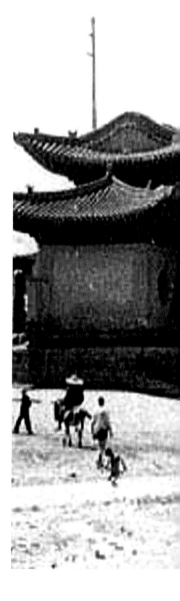

Left:
The covered corridor of the Santiao Bridge, Taishun, Zhejiang, is reminiscent of the wooden framework of common houses or temples. On the other hand, the underlying lifting structure is comprised of three sets of timber chords.

Above:
Said to have been built in the Tang dynasty, the Wo (Reclining or Holding) Bridge in Lanzhou, Gansu, served as a river crossing on the Silk Road. This mid-twentieth century photograph shows the bridge as it was restored in 1904, long before it became the prototype model for the Baling Bridge in Weiyuan.

Right:
Taken at the end of the nineteenth century, this covered bridge has an open pavilion atop it. Weizhou, Sichuan.

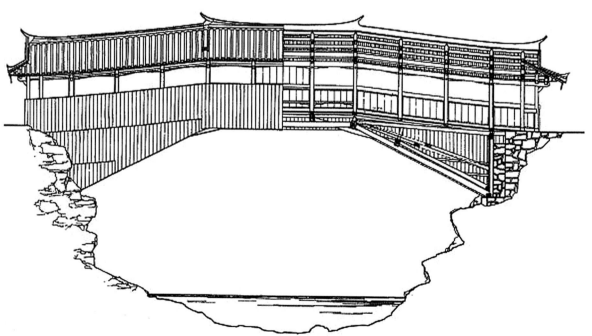

Above:
Long timbers laid horizontally on the stone abutments provide support for this modest covered bridge in the Sichuan countryside, which was photographed at the end of the nineteenth century.

Pages 52–3:
Structurally a cantilevered timber bridge rather than a woven timber arch bridge, the Baling Bridge in Gansu is regarded as a "rainbow bridge."

Top:
The Buchan (Stepping Toad) Bridge in Qingyuan county, Zhejiang, was first built between 1403 and 1424 and then rebuilt in 1917. Its single stone arch has a diameter of 17.8 meters while the corridor bridge itself has a length of 51.6 meters. Fifty meters away from the bridge is a stone in the water that is said to resemble the fabled toad in the moon, which led to the belief that one could reach the moon by crossing this bridge.

Above left:
The Yingjie Temple Bridge in Jushui township, Qingyuan county, Zhejiang, is adjacent to a temple built during the Song dynasty, rebuilt in 1662, and then restored in 1850 to its current state.

Above:
Modest covered bridges like this one in Fujian are found throughout southern China, where they provide not only easy passage over a stream but also offer a place for farmers and travelers to rest.

Right:
The 15.1-meter-long Sanzhu (Three Posts) Bridge, Zhejiang, has a clear span of 10.1 meters. The horizontal logs that support the timber frame corridor are held up by three stone pillars sunk into the streambed.

Good examples of covered bridges of many types are found throughout southern Zhejiang and northern Fujian provinces. Taishun and Qingyuan counties in mountainous Zhejiang share characteristics with the neighboring Fujian counties of Pingnan, Shouning, Zhouning, Gutian, Fu'an, and Fuding, each of which has a large number of striking covered bridges.

Only three stone columns hold up the timber assemblage supporting the Sanzhu Bridge, a relatively short covered bridge, 15.4 meters long, in Xia Wuyang village in Taishun. Also in Taishun is the 36-meter-long two-storey Yongqing Bridge, whose structure includes a piled cantilever timber beam bridge set upon a single midstream pier. Just upstream of the Yongqing Bridge, one can still see the chiseled-out indentations in the rocky bottom of the stream into which a set of pillars once supported a precursor bridge. Although its origins are unknown—it was last restored in 1916—the covered corridor of the Buchan Bridge in Qingyuan county was constructed over a massive single stone arch. Built above a smaller stone arch, the Yuwen Bridge is sited well among old trees and a rambling stream. A path paved with smooth stones drops from the adjacent hillsides, suggesting that the bridge is an anchor site in a system of mountain–valley byways. The imposing set of altars on the upper level of the bridge affirms its centrality in village worship. The Yingjie Temple Bridge in Qingyuan county is adjacent to one of the oldest extant temples in the region, which was built during the Song dynasty and then rebuilt in 1662. Also a two-storied bridge structure, the Yingjie Temple Bridge spans a narrow stream atop a series of long, parallel logs. Richly ornamented inside, the bridge continues as a vital community center. Among the most outstanding covered bridges in Shouning is the Luanfeng Bridge in Xiadang township. Built first in 1800 and restored in 1964, the bridge has a clear span of 37.6 meters, the greatest of any timber bridge in China, and an overall length of 47.6 meters and width of 4.9 meters. Among other notable covered bridges are the Yongqing Bridge, Liuzhai Bridge, and Dongguan Bridge, each with its own local characteristics.

In terms of internal building structure, only a relatively small number of covered bridges utilize masonry walls for the enclosed structure, an example of which can be seen on pages 208–11. As in dwellings and temples throughout China, the pillars-and-transverse-tie beams wooden framework, called *chuandou* in Chinese, and the column-and-beam construction, the *tailiang* framing system, are used in constructing bridges. Both of these wooden framework systems directly lift the roof. The pillars-and-transverse-tie beams wooden framework is common throughout southern China, and has been utilized in the Buchan, Yuwen, and Luanfeng bridges. This framing system is characterized by pillars of a relatively small diameter, with each of the slender pillars set on a stone base and notched at the top to directly support a longitudinal roof purlin. Horizontal tie beam members, called *chuanfang*, are mortised directly into or tenoned through the pillars in order to inhibit skewing of what would otherwise be a relatively flexible frame. Wooden components, as will be seen in many photographs, are linked together by

mortise-and-tenoned joinery, practices that can be traced back 7,000 years to Neolithic sites in eastern China. Column-and-beam construction involves a stacking of larger building parts: a horizontal beam, large in diameter and often curved, with two squat queen posts, or struts, set symmetrically upon it, followed by another beam and a culminating short post. Bracket sets are frequently used to extend the eaves substantially beyond the walls of the bridge.

The Yingjie Temple Bridge utilizes the *tailiang* framing system, with heavier and more substantial columns as well as large horizontal beams.

Timber frameworks of this type create a kind of "osseous" structure analogous to the human skeleton, which allows great flexibility, including structures that rise and fall as well as those comprising multiple levels. Because many covered bridges in China are also the sites of a shrine or temple, the roof structures are often

Above:
Built in 1797, the Yongqing (Eternal Celebration) Bridge in Taishun county, Zhejiang, is a cantilevered bridge with piled timbers laid atop its single midstream pier. With a length of 36 meters, the bridge rises 5.2 meters above the streambed.

Top:
Placed in a repeating fashion, sets of pillars and beams support the roof of the Yongqing Bridge.

Above:
Midway across the corridor, a set of wooden steps leads to the loft containing a variety of deities on several altars.

more elaborate than those found on homes and are more like the roofs of temples. Ceiling structures are quite varied, especially near shrines and altars, where elaborately carved and painted coffered forms are common. With sawn timber cladding, the walling on bridges is generally simpler than that found on dwellings and temples.

Much like the practices adopted in building houses, units of the wooden framework are assembled on the ground before being raised to a perpendicular location, where they are then propped and secured to adjacent segments by longitudinal cross members. As with Chinese house building, the raising of the ridgepole as well as some of the columns are important steps that are accompanied with ritual. With shrines and altars, covered bridges are transformed into active sites of worship, a subject discussed and illustrated on pages 72–5.

Garden Bridges

While the term "garden" in the West brings with it the notion of a relatively diminutive space with landscaped elements and structures created essentially for pleasure, this is only partially true in China. Here, gardens include not only small private gardens of literati scholars but also large imperial complexes that sometimes are as much administrative headquarters and parks as gardens. Monastery and temple precincts, imperial tombs as well as sprawling natural areas such as are found around Xihu, West Lake, in Hangzhou, may also be considered today as gardens. In all of these areas, there was an ingenious reproduction and spatial interplay of mountains, streams, ponds, trees, and rockeries as well as carefully designed structures such as halls, pavilions, galleries, and, of course, bridges.

In the canal-laced Jiangnan region in the lower reaches of the Chang Jiang or Yangzi River, many towns and cities are renowned for their literati gardens, sites for contemplation, study, and the cultivation of plants. As later chapters will show, bridges in these gardens provide passage but also offer invitations to tarry and ponder the meaning of poetic allusions embodied in buildings and natural vistas. Lined with low balustrades, simple stone beam bridges seem to rest on the water so that one can enjoy the lotus plants and the swimming fish. Zigzag bridges help extend the appreciation of a compact space by augmenting the distance between two points. Arch bridges have a scale and charm that invites one to pause and enjoy a view from above. In Yangzhou, the Wuting Bridge, also called the Five Pavilions Bridge and the Lotus

Left:
Taken just outside Shanghai's Yuyuan Garden, this late nineteenth century photograph shows the fabled zigzag bridge and teahouse with its upturned eaves, which is said to have been the inspiration for the blue-and-white willow pattern porcelain exported from China to England during the last half of the eighteenth century.

Below left:
Looking back from the teahouse across a wooden version of the zigzag bridge, the viewer sees the low-rise buildings and narrow lanes of the old walled city of Shanghai.

Bottom and right:
These contemporary views of the teahouse and zigzag bridge reveal in the distance the futuristic skyline of modern Pudong. In pools such as this one, teeming goldfish are believed to keep the water from stagnating, thus promoting the movement of positive *qi*, the life-giving force.

Flower Bridge because of its resemblance to the open petals of the flower, is as much a pavilion as it is a bridge, a magnificent structure of substantial scale.

While the imperial gardens, hunting preserves, and parks in and around capitals such as Chang'an and Kaifeng have all been destroyed, existing only in literary texts, paintings, and memory, Beijing, which served as the imperial capital of the Ming and Qing dynasties for more than 500 years, is enriched with many fine examples. These include what came to be known as the "Western Seas," the linked southern, middle, and northern lakes along the western side of the walled Purple Forbidden City. Although these interconnected bodies of water have few bridges, several are distinctive and can be contrasted with smaller spaces with bridges within the walls of the palace complex. Today, in the northwestern suburbs of Beijing, it is possible to visit and appreciate some of the imperial garden complexes that developed especially in the eighteenth century but suffered grievously during the middle to late nineteenth century, only to be reborn in the century that followed.

Known as "Garden of Gardens," this area includes not only the vestigial remains of the once glorious Yuanming Yuan but also the grand Yihe Yuan, known to Westerners as the Summer Palace, a late nineteenth-century reconstruction reborn through the efforts of the Empress Dowager Cixi. The disposition of hills, causeways, canals, and islands connected to Kunming Lake made possible the creation of some thirty bridges, some imposingly grand and others quietly simple. Imitating the famed Su Causeway along the western side of West Lake in Hangzhou, is a causeway along the west side of Kunming Lake replete with six bridges, four of which are capped with pavilions. "Borrowing" scenes from the surrounding hills and sky beyond, just as with much smaller gardens in southern China, bridges were sited to capture the vistas and serve as a component of a panoramic scene as well. Perhaps the most elegant is the Yudai (Jade Belt) Bridge, a humpbacked feature that rises high like a breaking wave. On the opposite side of the lake is the magnificent Seventeen Arches Bridge that reposes like a symmetrical 150-meter-long rainbow as it rises slowly to a crescendo before diminishing. Hundreds of carved lion figures sit atop the balusters of the bridge. Clearly examples of human ingenuity and artistic sensitivity, these bridges continue to inspire the poetic imaginations of visitors, stirring images and reminiscences that link them to the interwoven fabric of China's enduring civilization.

In integrating the rational and functional with the romantic and aesthetic, the anonymous builders of most of China's bridges created tangible links across voids that, to poets, speak of "rainbows lying on the waves" and "turtles' backs reaching the clouds." Joseph Needham was hardly exaggerating when he suggested that "No Chinese bridge lacked beauty and many were remarkably beautiful" (1971: 145). Viewing Chinese bridges as architectural structures provides opportunities to comment on Chinese technology, connections with Western engineering developments, and aesthetic traditions.

Above:
Viewed by many as China's most glorious bridge, the Shiqigong (Seventeen Arches) Bridge in the Yihe Yuan or Summer Palace in Beijing, rises like a rainbow in a gentle 150-meter-long arc.

Far left:
The Bridge of the Twenty-four in Yangzhou was sited so that it is one element in a composition that not only includes nearby water and a pavilion but also "borrowed" scenery beyond, with trees and a pagoda.

Left:
At the end of the nineteenth century when this photograph of the Bridge of Nine Bends at the heart of West Lake in Hangzhou was taken, the complex known as Lesser Yingzhou Isle was much as it was in 1607 when it was created—a lake within a lake and an island within an island—using mud dredged from the bottom. Substantial expansion took place beginning in 1982 to reach its current extent.

Pages 62–3:
Rising like a camel's back or a surging wave, the white marble Yudai (Jade Belt) Bridge in Beijing's Yihe Yuan or Summer Palace, is one of China's most beautiful structures.

Sichuan Garden Parks

Unlike the compact metropolitan gardens of the Jiang-nan region, characterized by cleverly dense yet elegant compositions of specific elements and an internal focus, the gardens in the Chengdu Plain of western Sichuan tend to sprawl loosely, with rugged, even primitive, elements. Reminiscent of what is known of the evolution of ancient imperial parks and gardens, which Jerome Silbergeld characterizes as vast zoological, botanical, and geological "theme parks" (2004: 208), to later expansive imperial estates, Sichuan gardens preserve an open-style design of loose and fluid components, with an emphasis on water and relatively flat terrain. Rockery, unlike in Jiangnan gardens, is essentially absent, with hills and mountains only glimpsed from afar. Dense bamboo groves, overarching trees, and dark surfaces together project a rustic primitiveness. It is within this natural context that bridges of many types are situated, a good many of which appear as if deposited there by nature—logs fallen across a rivulet, cobblestones deposited after a flood. Good examples are found in the park-like setting for the thatched cottage of Du Fu, the renowned seventh-century poet, where the sculpting and shaping of the overall site and the assembled placement of bridges, water, and associated buildings evoke the naturalism of earlier times in China and an aesthetic that some see even as Japanese. Once-private gardens in Sichuan have evolved into public parks that memorialize the region's noted historical figures.

Top, above, and right:
This sprawling public garden in Chengdu, Sichuan, centers on the heralded *caotang* or thatched cottage of Du Fu, a Tang-dynasty poet. It is said that Du Fu chose this location near Huanhua Xi (Washing Flowers Creek) because of its simple beauty. With dense vegetation, including groves of bamboo, the naturalistic garden differs significantly from better known gardens in the Jiangnan region. Paths lead to as well as help define distinctive areas of the garden. Although none of the bridges is ancient, each, as these images show, is a relatively simply composition of stone, wood, and bamboo laid simply as planks or aligned in a zigzag shape.

Historical and Modern Bridges

Over the past two decades, some of the world's most daring and beautiful bridges have been built in China, achievements essentially unknown in the West. While new bridges in Shanghai, Hong Kong, Guangzhou, and a few other large cities are well known, countless other fine bridges have been completed as components of the country's explosive development of its overall transportation infrastructure. These include innovative engineering approaches that have challenged the structural status quo, including girder bridges that receive some support from cables and even some "next generation" structures that seemingly defy accepted engineering principles and basic physics. Not surprisingly, as elsewhere in the world, the international media reports on failures, such as the Fenghuang Bridge in Hunan, whose collapse in 2007 was attributed to contractors cutting corners, but rarely highlights the extraordinary medium-scale and smaller modern bridges being built throughout the country.

Old China hands remember well the national pride accompanying the completion, in December 1968, of the Yangzi River Bridge at Nanjing, a majestic double-decker, double-track highway and railway bridge, which Western engineers had claimed would be impossible to build at the site. Today, there are more than fifty bridges spanning the Yangzi, with another sixty planned to be added by 2020, each one deemed necessary in order to nurture interregional trade. The Chinese press heralds the completion of each new bridge in terms of originality and importance, many of which are world class. Shanghai's Lupu Bridge over the Huangpu River, opened in 2003, which has a main span of 550 meters, is the world's longest arch bridge. In eastern Zhejiang province, the Xihoumen Bridge, now the second longest suspension bridge in the world, was completed in December 2007, overtaking the Runyang Bridge linking Yangzhou and Zhenjiang in

2003, which at the time was China's longest suspension bridge. In the summer of 2007, the Hangzhou Bay Bridge became the longest transoceanic bridge in the world, although it does not have the longest cable-stayed main span; it is expected to be open to traffic in 2008. A feasibility study has been carried out to build an even longer cross-sea suspension bridge across the Qiongzhou Straits between Guangdong and Hainan provinces. The completion of new structures in provinces and counties is always a time to savor—and boast about—the technical, economic, and aesthetic significance of bridge building.

Spurred by the need to rebuild and refashion China's large, medium, and small towns and cities, planners and architects have brought about a transformation of urban landscapes, including not only the development of transportation infrastructure but also the expansion of green spaces, including parks as well as tree-lined roads, canals, and streams. Such developments, unfortunately, have brought in their wake the well-documented and tragic destruction of cultural landscapes, including the demolition of countless old houses, neighborhoods, temples, and bridges, all in the name of progress. As is well known, moreover, environmental degradation has fouled the air and

Above:
While this structure appears like an open spandrel bridge, it is in fact a fanciful and imposing arched entry to a new development in Chengdu, Sichuan.

Below:
Located in an expanded western garden of the Yihe Yuan or Summer Palace in Beijing, this new bridge mimics the form of the original Zhaozhou Bridge.

Right:
The Anshun (Peaceful and Favorable) Bridge, completed in 2003 to replace a bridge lost in a flood in the 1980s, straddles the Jinjiang River and provides space for a restaurant in the revitalized downtown area of Chengdu, Sichuan.

water over much of China at a scale that is intolerable, increasing dangers to the health and quality of life of hundreds of millions of people. At the same time, even in a city as polluted as Beijing, the investment in green spaces has led to the restoration of cultural heritage as well as the creation of ersatz historical landscapes.

While the inherited built environment is indeed a resource that can stimulate economic progress and nurture historical awareness, sadly much conservation work has been crude, management unsatisfactory, and collateral damage from explosive commercial expansion substantial. On the other hand, as will be seen in several portions of this book, such as with the Zhaozhou Bridge, the Lugou Bridge, and the Feng or Maple Bridge, just to mention a few examples, important old bridges have become the anchors of reasonably well-maintained tourist sites. In Taishun and Qingyuan counties in Zhejiang and Shouning county in Fujian—both areas of clean water and blue skies—the large collections of distinctive covered wooden bridges are seen as unique resources to be restored as magnets to draw visitors. Parks also increasingly are being used as safe repositories for bridges and buildings removed from other locations. Sometimes, the fact that a structure is a transplant is noted on a sign, but all too often visitors are left to assume that they are seeing historic structures in situ. As the photographs on this page also reveal, showy, faux historical bridges are being built to serve as civic icons. In Zhengzhou, Henan, a

theme park based on Zhang Zeduan's eleventh-century *Qingming shanghe tu* handscroll, has as its centerpiece the painting's celebrated rainbow bridge.

Inspired by the country's splendid indigenous bridge building traditions and rushing to meet infrastructure needs, Chinese engineers and architects push the frontiers of twenty-first century materials, technologies, and standards to create functional and beautiful bridges. This is, in many ways, reminiscent of earlier, quieter times of less hurried change when similarly daring and beautiful bridges were built.

Below:
In the Maple Bridge Scenic Area in Suzhou, the restoration of the old arched bridge and other buildings has been accompanied by the construction of new bridges, such as this gallery bridge, as ways to disperse visitors and to offer them a richer experience.

Part Two

CHINESE BRIDGES AS LIVING ARCHITECTURE

BRIDGES AND FOLK CULTURE

Until recent times, no other architectural form in China seemed so mute—even invisible—as bridges. Temples, monasteries, palaces, pagodas, tombs, and shrines, even houses—all with obvious tales to tell—readily draw the attention of scholars in many fields who read the "meaning" of their layouts and iconography. However, bridges have rarely been analyzed in any way that goes beyond the mechanics of their construction, emphasizing lines and materials, and that highlight their aesthetics. However, a cursory examination of old bridges reveals that most are emblazoned with significant elements whose meaning surpasses mere ornamentation. Decorative elements, of course, are not common on simple wood or stone beam bridges, but, as structural components rise above the deck—posts, capitals, panels, and balustrades—decorative elements multiply just as they do in and about halls, palaces, verandas, houses, terraces, and gates. Where the bridge is topped with a structure to become a covered bridge—the number of which in China is truly staggering—the gallery becomes a temple with the same range of iconographic elements found in any other temple. Much of the trimming on bridges shares motifs with other architectural forms, such as palaces and temples, but some are distinctive to bridges because they relate to the calming of waters and the protection against flood. Moreover, larger bridges—as with any Chinese building—usually are built with careful attention to all of the common elements of *fengshui* in order to influence—even insure— the fate of the community within which they stand.

Some meaningful aspects of a bridge are introduced as the materials are collected to build it on a site that has been carefully considered. Other features emerge, sometimes quite slowly as financial resources permit or more quickly during a period of efflorescence when significant resources are expended in rebuilding. Some ornamentation endures because it was carved in stone or wood, while others are only periodically obvious as they appear and reappear as the seasons change. In some cases, the meaning of the imagery is lost because the conditions that made it evident are forgotten or lay latent because it is overlain with newer elements.

The commonly heard phrase "where there is a bridge, there is a temple; where there is a temple, there is a bridge" points to the centrality of devotion associated with a building that might at first blush only seem to be a route of passage across the water. Throughout the more developed areas of China, however, once-common shrines and temples—not only related to bridges but also those in rural and urban neighborhoods generally—have been substantially eradicated over the years because of political campaigns and even disinterest. In newly reconstructed bridges, sometimes only an empty wooden case or a small brick structure that once held gods and the paraphernalia of worship are seen. Still, in the countryside, it is common to find shrines and altars on, within, and adjacent to old bridges, the variety of which resonates the rich diversity of religious traditions in China. Moreover, the role of monks in soliciting contributions and in the actual design and construction of bridges is noteworthy. Because of the interconnections between bridges and religion, especially local folk beliefs but also Buddhism, this topic is explored.

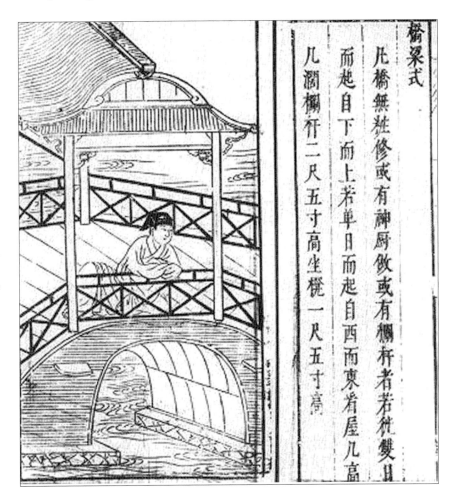

Fengshui and Building Magic

Just as in the quest for an auspicious location for a house, grave, garden, and temple, no bridge of any significance was positioned without attention to *fengshui*, which is rooted in the conscious selection of a "site"—the actual space occupied by the bridge—and its "situation"—the location of the site in relation to its broader surroundings. The search for a suitable, even ideal and optimal spatial setting for a bridge has always taken considerable time as has the selection of actual building materials, such as stone and wood. When coupled with bridge building rituals and protective amulets, *fengshui* contributed substantially to assuring villagers and townspeople of a secure and happy life in its environs.

Less is known about the application of *fengshui* practices in the building of bridges in northern China than in southern China, where meandering streams and undulating hills offer myriad components amenable to consideration by *fengshui* masters—"interpreters of wind and water"—of the Configurations School, with their concern for optimizing landscape configurations. The inherent beauty of many of the sites for old bridges in southern China calls attention to what once were thoughtful and careful deliberations. Many bridges are located at a site called *shuikou*, literally the "mouth of water," where the stream exits from the settlement. In this thinking, the bridge is able to hold back wealth in a village

so that it does not flow away. Indeed, as a settlement, grows beyond the location of a bridge, the bridge may be dismantled and moved downstream where it can serve the same blocking purpose. A good example is the Bajiang (Eight Rivers) Bridge in Sanjiang county, Guangxi, which was taken apart, piece by piece, and then rebuilt some 400 meters downstream. If a *shuikou* is judged too wide, then the building of a bridge will contribute to a contraction of the water's exit, an improvement in the overall condition. Sinuous mountains are often metaphorically described as a "dragon" or *long*, whose body is an undulating yet

Above:
The Bajiang (Eight Rivers) Bridge in Sanjiang, Guangxi, was taken apart and then rebuilt some 400 meters downstream in order to "prevent wealth from leaving the growing town." This view shows the piers of the old bridge in the foreground and the reconstructed bridge at a new location in the distance, where it serves its "blocking" function to keep the town prosperous.

interconnected organism that may be extensive and complex or rather simple. In understanding the specific location of some of the soaring covered "rainbow bridges" of southern Zhejiang and northern Fujian, villagers describe the line of the bridge as actually materially completing a segment of a dragon's body draped across the hillslopes.

In addition to determining the optimal spatial positioning of a bridge, attention was also paid to the temporal dimension—propitious timing—of all building activities. Almanacs have always included notations about auspicious dates, as with other buildings, for beginning the construction of bridges in general. When the bridge is a covered structure with building members like those of a house or temple, the selection of auspicious dates and hours to fell timbers for ridgepoles and columns is carefully considered. Careful thought was given to how the carpenter's trestle was placed as well as how wood was shaped within it. Ritual attended critical junctures in bridge building: raising the initial columns and beams to give shape to the central bay, determining the slope of the roof, and hoisting the ridgepole.

Left:
The 1843 Xianju Bridge in Taishun county, Zhejiang, was sited so that its rising arched shape would connect portions of an undulating series of ridges that serve metaphorically as a "dragon" or *long*.

Above left:
Protective amulets, like this one affixed to the Yongqing Bridge, Taishun county, Zhejiang, include symbols such as the *bagua*, *taiji*, readable Chinese characters, and indecipherable Daoist spirit text.

Above right:
It is common to see a *taiji* symbol as well as inscribed auspicious characters written on the underside of a ridgepole above the central bay of a covered bridge. Sanjiang county, northern Guangxi.

Below left, bottom, and right:
Timing, ritual, and the use of amulets have traditionally been important considerations in settling on a suitable log to become the ridgepole of a new bridge, whose strength was critical in supporting the weight of the bridge, once the actual site for the new bridge had been determined. Below are three essential steps in the process: selecting the tree in the forest, felling the tree, and finally carrying the log to the building site.

The complete building of a bridge, the Tongle Bridge in Taishun county, Zhejiang, took place over a 26-month period in 2004–6 as each step was governed by calendrical decision making, with the high point being *shangliang*, the raising of the ridgepole. This ritual, as with houses and temples, involves the chanting of rhymed "luck bringing" verses and offerings of poultry, *ji*, that is homophonous with "good luck," and a basket containing the five grains, incense, steamed buns, as well as other food and wine. Hanging from ridgepoles of many old and new bridges in southern China is a wrapped pair of chopsticks, invoking hopes for fertility and prosperity, because of the homophonous association linking the word for chopsticks, *kuaizi*, with "sons coming quickly." Within any old covered bridge, if one glances up at the ridgepole or pays careful attention to some of the columns, it is possible to see the residuum of past ritual, arcane characters inscribed directly on the timbers or hung from paper attached to them. These usually include combined *taiji* and *bagua* symbols as antispectral charms. Today, moreover, one sometimes stumbles across an incomplete covered bridge, seemingly abandoned, but actually only temporarily in a state of suspension until the next appropriate "lucky" day arrives to move on to the next step in the building process. When the bridge is finally completed, a concluding auspicious day must be determined to hold a ceremony of completion, including an expansive banquet, for all of the workers as well as those in the community who contributed to the bridge's construction. In November 2006, we witnessed the celebration accompanying the extension of the bays of the wooden framework of a covered bridge atop a concrete bridge in northern Guangzi. Replete with costumed

Pages 70 and 73–5:
The fourteen bridge building images on these pages are a small selection from hundreds taken over a 26-month period in 2004–6 by Xue Yichuan, a young photographer who documented each of the steps carried out by carpenters and ritual specialists in building the Tongle Bridge in Taishun county, Zhejiang. Each step—from selecting and felling the tree in the forest, carrying the log, shaping the timber, adding auspicious symbols while it rested in a trestle frame, offering sacrifices before and then raising the ridgepole, setting off firecrackers, preparing a feast of a whole hog for the carpenters, and having a a Daoist priest conduct a completion ceremony—was governed by auspicious dates and times. As with houses and temples, rituals involved the chanting of rhymed "luck bringing" verses and offering a basket containing the five grains, incense, steamed buns, food and wine, and a chicken, called *ji* in Chinese and homophonous with "good luck."

elders, a whole roasted pig, fighting water buffalos, and endlessly noisy firecrackers, the activity was truly a marvellous community event.

Besides being sited according to *fengshui* principles, a bridge also traditionally became a *fengshui* object, whose presence itself insured good fortune for the villagers, especially the prominent families who supported its construction. If a bridge were to weaken, even fall into disrepair, many would see this as a sign of the likely decline of the village and its inhabitants as well. It is no wonder then that genealogies give prominence to the charitable works of a family, tracing as well the interdependence of fortune and landscape features. The siting of a bridge at a stream crossing, like the siting of a pagoda on a hill or a resting pavilion or memorial arch along a path, inserted material objects that embellished a landscape and helped demarcate its beauty. This is also true of the presence of an ancient cypress or banyan tree, with gnarled roots and rugged bark, or a *fengshui* wood made up of pine trees—all symbols of longevity. A nearby shrine to the Earth God or some other spirit alongside a bridgehead adds a mystical element. These are all found commonly together enough to underscore that there indeed is a mutual positive

complementarity in the scripting of sublime landscapes with the bridge as the unifying focus. On the other hand, the stark presence today of modern roads, buildings, and even bridges—all comparatively crudely inserted into the landscape—stand in contrast to the coordinated and sensitive decision making often characteristic of *fengshui*.

Buddhism and Bridge Building

The building and maintenance of bridges traditionally was the responsibility of local magistrates, although some larger bridges were built using imperial resources. Indeed, Mencius included bridges among the ways a magistrate showed concern for the welfare of people by doing good works: "If the footbridges are built by the eleventh month and the carriage bridges by the twelfth month every year, the people will not suffer the hardship of fording" (Lau, 1984: 128). Later, a Qing magistrate "could be punished with a year's loss of salary if an important bridge in his jurisdiction collapsed, and lashed thirty strokes if he failed to repair a dilapidated bridge" (Kieschnick, 2003: 209). Magistrates, aware of their responsibility, however, still required a trustworthy individual or organization to facilitate the efforts.

Records reveal that magistrates usually called on local Buddhist monks not only to accumulate the funds but also to arrange for materials and labor, sometimes even to carry out the design and actual construction. But why monks? John Kieschnick outlines five reasons spelled out by a Song-dynasty author: "Monks are devoted to helping others and hence willing to work tirelessly; monks have developed powerful capacities of concentration (through meditation) and hence do not abandon a project before it is completed; a monk is not burdened by wife or children and hence does not keep money for his family; monks believe in the principle of karmic retribution and hence are not corrupt; because the monk is devoted to the task, great men support him and lesser men follow him" (p. 206).

Monks thus served as linking connections between local government and individuals and families who had the capacity to be actual donors. Community élites often were the objects of solicitations of financial support for public works like bridges and roads in addition to community facilities such as temples and academies. Major donors were assured of the importance of their compassionate philanthropy: a necessary task would be accomplished that would benefit the public at large and, sometimes more importantly, as an act of piety "the good would be rewarded through the Buddhist mechanism of merit of which bridge-building was a part" (p. 213). Of course, with charitable acts, there no doubt usually were an assortment of motives and a panoply of incentives, some altruistic and benevolent and some selfish and self-serving.

Be this as it may, bridges of incalculable number got built and maintained because of the mutual interdependence of a triangle of individuals—magistrates-monks-donors. Stone steles were usually carved to memorialize the narrative of giving and accomplishment, often alongside subsidiary steles with a detailed accounting of every contribution made from near and far. The repetition of surnames and association of given names sometimes reveal the power of a local lineage, where each of the specific amounts of the individual contributions by patrons is listed clearly. Many of these steles include Buddhist imagery and stock phrases relating to gaining merit. Set up at one of the bridgeheads, such steles over time came to provide a narrative of a community's role in the maintenance of a bridge as a public resource. Even today, the renovation of an old bridge or the building of a new one reflects a level of organization and recordkeeping that is remarkable. Throughout rural China, one can still witness the solicitation of funds in support of a bridge. Stone steles, wooden tablets, and paper banners register the names and specific amounts contributed by donors,

Far left:
Buddhist prayers written in Sanskrit and Chinese as well as small images of the Buddha are carved along the sides of this stupa on the Luoyang Bridge, Quanzhou, Fujian.

Left:
After the Beijian (Northern Stream) Bridge was built in 1674 and refurbished in 1849, the names of the original patrons were memorialized on these stone tablets. Taishun county, Zhejiang.

Left below:
Those who contributed to the recent restoration of the Yuwen (Nourish Culture) Bridge had their names written in ink on the board hung in the rafters. Taishun county, Zhejiang.

sometimes ranked in decreasing order according to the amount given and sometimes listed according to when the contributions were made. Today, corporate and government sponsors play important roles in funding some of the key bridges undergoing reconstruction. Although rare, it is even possible to encounter a monk or a village elder on some out-of-the-way bridge, sitting on a bench and soliciting passersby for small donations for the maintenance or rebuilding of the bridge.

Beyond the role of financial managers, there are many records that reveal that monks actually designed bridges themselves and were actively involved in arranging materials and labor as well as participating in construction work as carpenters and masons. Some of the best and most accessible documentation of this concerns the building of the megalithic stone bridges in Fujian, discussed on pages 212–17, where a number of well-known monks gained substantial experience as "engineers." Needham highlights the work of the monk Dao Xun, who during the thirteenth century is said to have built more than 200 bridges of many types, calling him and others "monastic technologists" (1971: 154–5). These megalithic stone bridges, as with many others bridges in China, were adorned with Buddhist syllables, iconography, and stupas in addition to statues of myriad deities and illustrated scriptural stories.

Right center:
With a history of more than 1,000 years, the Luoyang Bridge has had many contributors, many of whom are listed on stone stelae, today gathered together near an old temple. Quanzhou, Fujian.

Right:
This wooden plaque chronicles the many corporate and institutional contributions made to restore the Houkeng Bridge in Qingyuan county, Zhejiang.

Bridges and Worship

The association of bridges with temples and shrines is clearly deeply rooted in Chinese culture, even going beyond their construction being supervised by monks and the resources making them possible arising from a quest for merit by the faithful. Not only were bridges often built adjacent to temples and even inside their precincts, but temples were also frequently built on top of bridges in some areas. Sometimes the names of a bridge and a nearby temple or shrine were the same, a fact that underscores their interdependence.

Because of the tumult of the past century and a half in China, countless temples and shrines were, of course, obliterated with only a local place name echoing a past existence.

Many more bridges have been stripped of any of their religious elements, preserving simply a shell with the empty wooden case or small brick shrine that once held gods and the accouterments of worship now empty and the religious iconography chiseled off. Nonetheless, far away from major cities and towns, it is still common in the countryside—where the rich diversity of folk religious traditions in China continues to resonate—to see shrines and altars on, within, and adjacent to old bridges.

At one end of the famed Zhaozhou Bridge, there once was a large temple to Guandi, the God of War, but it stands empty today, just as is the case of many other

bridges. With little of colorful character of times past, a functioning, but rebuilt, temple rests at one end of the Baodai Bridge outside Suzhou. An immense temple sits at one end of the Wan'an Bridge in Pingnan county in Fujian. Its surviving woodcarvings are elaborate and rich with meaning even though many have been badly damaged, with faces chiseled off. The altar is tall and broad, no doubt once laden with numerous gods and goddesses as well as offerings. Today, only a few newly manufactured statues of no particular value rest relatively alone. On an island along the Wan'an Bridge in Quanzhou, Fujian, is a very active temple.

Perhaps nowhere are temples and shrines associated with bridges still found in such numbers as in the mountains of Fujian, Jiangxi, and Zhejiang provinces where folk religion is especially syncretistic. Here, in

Above, left, and above right: The Liuzhai (Lu Family) Bridge, built in 1405 and rebuilt in 1666, is a double-decker structure 18.4 meters long with a corridor bridge beneath and a full second-storey temple atop it. Accessible via a wooden stairway, the temple level is constructed of massive carved timber beams. Multiple altars and shrines are regularly visited by villagers.

Right and far right:
Adjacent to the Hongjun Bridge in Qinglinkou, Sichuan, is the Huoshen (Fire Spirit or Fire God) Temple, which enshrines Daoist deities who coexist with myriad Buddhist deities. Although there are no clergy, an elderly lady assists visitors by selling incense, candles, and paper money for them to burn as offerings. Since many visitors may not recognize the images, each has a sign indicating its name and significance.

the central portion of most covered bridges are altars to major gods in the Daoist or Buddhist pantheon as well as lesser local or regional gods. Some gods can be implored when a villager is facing illness or misfortune; some exist merely as intermediaries that can be prayed to when assistance is needed from a higher god. The wax drippings, darkened beams, and burnt incense suggest regular use. At one time, a stove for burning spirit money was beside every altar, but today, because of the fear of fire, most are placed outside the wooden structure. Some altars are attended, but most are not. Visitors can purchase candles or incense and deposit money into a box. There usually are cushions to kneel on. On the altar of some bridges, as in any temple, is a wooden container holding bamboo sticks, each one with a number and writing that represents an idea,

action, or suggestion. The one seeking advice shakes the container until one stick jumps out. This stick, which is said to be capable of indicating the future, has a number on it that corresponds with a poetic passage written on a sheet of paper hanging on the wall. While many of these gods and goddesses can be approached at any time, most receive special attention on the birthday of the god or goddess. On these special days, the image is removed from the shrine and set into a wooden palanquin, usually stored in the rafters above the altar, and then carried in a noisy procession before the doors of all families in a village. The cycle of the agricultural calendar in Fujian, Jiangxi, and Zhejiang once was replete with dates to celebrate the gods and goddesses. Today, for the most part, these practices no longer occur with the frequency of past times.

While most altars are inserted in a bay at the middle of a covered bridge or in a shrine at the end of the bridge, there are many bridges with a separate space for worship on a second level at the heart of the bridge. Yuwen Bridge in Zhouling township in Taishun is an exquisite open wooden structure built atop a stone base with a single arch. Shaded by a pair of old trees, a gnarled camphor and a pine, as well as framed by the large boulders of a narrow ravine,

Top:
The megalithic Anping Bridge in Jinjiang, Fujian, built between 1138 and 1151, has an historical association with a large, prosperous temple complex located midway across the bridge's 2070-meter-long span. Today, the span is accessible by vehicles via a roadway as well as on foot across the bridge. Near by the Anping Bridge are numerous smaller shrines.

Above left and right:
Built in the 1600s, the Baiyun Bridge in Qingyuan, Zhejiang province, is only 8.34 meters long, with a glass-encased altar featuring Guanyin, the Goddess of Mercy, along one of its walls.

the site is indeed magical. It has a surprisingly large devotional space in a loft above the main gallery, all capped with a triple-eaved roof. Accessible via a ladder, the main altar is to Wenchang Di, the "Emperor of Prospering Culture," also known as the God of Literature, a stern supernatural official who exemplifies morality. A pair of faithful boy attendants, one named Tianlong, meaning "born deaf," and the other Diya, meaning "born mute," accompanies him. It is said that he intentionally employs two handicapped boys since the one who can hear cannot speak, while the other can speak but cannot hear, thus insuring confidence.

Near to many bridges there are places for lay individuals to set free live creatures, a practice that is called *fangsheng* in Chinese. Some bridges identified with such customs are named Fangsheng Bridge, which can be translated as Liberate Living Things Bridge. Among the most famous is Fangsheng Bridge in the center of Zhujiajiao town in the suburbs of Shanghai. Built by the monk Xing Chao in 1571, this 72-meter-long five-arch stone bridge rises 7.4 meters above the Grand Canal. Xing Chao also established a *fangsheng she*, an organization whose purpose was to "liberate living things" following the Buddhist admonition, "Among all negative karma, that of killing is the heaviest. Among all positive karma, that for releasing life is the highest." A small area at the foot of the bridge, where no one was permitted to fish, was situated for the pious to come and set free fish, turtles, and even birds—some of which might have been bought in a nearby market—in order to gain merit. Today, visitors can purchase from old ladies transparent

plastic bags filled with water and goldfish. Once the fish slip back into the water, the individual setting them free is said to gain merit. Throughout the town, inscriptions remind townsfolk that liberating animals and doing good deeds are compassionate acts that help one accumulate merit.

Protective Amulets

There is no documented evidence that carpenters or masons involved in bridge building in the past employed the kind of "building magic" common with house building (Knapp, 2005: 109–31). It is nonetheless possible that those responsible for bridge building sometimes had to counter whatever sorcery was employed by carpenters or masons unhappy with their payment or treatment, in order to "protect" the bridge and those using it from such malicious efforts. Prophylactic amulets and actions have always been an important preventative measure taken in building in China.

On many bridges there are protective amulets whose purpose is the "calming of the waters," essentially protection against floodwaters that too often rise quickly. In particular, dragons and *taotie*, the latter a mythical, ferocious-looking beast with a head but no body and said to be the benign offspring of the dragon, have been seen as having an efficacy against dangers inherent with running water because of their mere presence. Dragons, of course, represent but one manifestation of a creature the Chinese have held to be truly magical and that exists in many configurations. Indeed, the mythological connotations of Chinese dragons are manifold, as are their sizes and shapes and how they are portrayed. Besides being common symbols of good luck and symbolic of imperial power, some of the nine types of dragons traditionally were believed to have utilitarian functions in regard to water. While the spirit

Top:
Said to be one of the nine offspring of the dragon, this *taotie*-like totem, which inspires awe and terror, is found on the middle balustrade panel on the Zhaozhou Bridge in Hebei province.

Above:
Dragons, here playfully intertwined, are common and varied motifs on the Zhaozhou Bridge, Hebei.

dragon or *shenlong* lived in the sky and had the capacity to bring needed rain, the *jiaolong* or water dragon, sometimes called the flood dragon, ruled over underground springs and surface water, inhabiting as it did deep pools of water.

According to popular legend, Emperor Yu, about 2205 BCE, while engaged in curbing the great flood that scourged the country, had the assistance of a dragon to map out waterways with its writhing tail. Endowed with the ability to summon clouds and bring forth rain as well as control floods that causes destruction and death, the dynamic dragon represented a beneficent power. In averting drought, providing needed water, thus insuring a good harvest, a dragon contributed to the stability of the empire. The dragon, it was said, usually appeared with the spring equinox, the time of planting, and descended into its chasm to rest at the autumn equinox, the end of the flood season. Throughout southern China especially, three-dimensional writhing dragons are positioned as totems above the ridgepole as well as on paintings within the galleries of covered bridges. On the Fangsheng Bridge in Zhujiajiao, near Shanghai, are stone tablets called Dragon Gate stones, which are engraved with eight coiling dragons encircling a shining pearl.

It is doubtful that any bridge reveals richer and more beautiful protective imagery than that found on the Zhaozhou Bridge in Hebei. On each side of the roadway, the parapet incorporates twenty-two stone posts, many carved with stylized coiled dragons and

topped with a finial composed of a bamboo section, a pearl, or a sitting lion. Of the twenty-one carved balustrades, four at the center of the bridge are dominated by meandering *jiaolong* or water dragons. Covered with scales, a clear indication that they inhabit the water rather than the sky, most of the dragons writhe singly or in pairs. One dragon playfully passes through a hole in one panel before reappearing on another panel. The face of a dragon carved in high relief appears on the center balustrade on each side.

When reflected in the river beneath, the symmetrical image of the Zhaozhou Bridge itself is viewed by some as an abstract form of the supernatural *taotie*. The open spandrels, according to this view, suggest the *taotie*'s fixed open eyes, while the sweeping curve of the segmental arch recalls its gaping jaws. According to a Song poem, the grimacing and gluttonous *taotie*-like bridge stands ready "to kill the anger of the flood" by devouring the gushing water, much as the use of the Chinese character *tun*, meaning to "devour," is sometimes seen written on a mirror above a door to a house.

Found on many other bridges on the north China plain is a stylized carved animal mask on the keystone. Thought by some to be in the shape of a *chiwen*, another spawn of the dragon, figures of this sort are also carved on the roof ridges of buildings as a defense against fire. On the beams of bridges, their appearance reflects their fondness for water. As powerful representative forms, the dragon and the many guises of its offspring clearly serve as protective amulets.

Auspicious Emblems

No bridge is embellished with more lions than the Lugou Bridge in Wanping, Beijing. While popular lore says that the lions are countless and extremely varied, some 485 indeed have been counted. Most sit atop individual capitals along the balustrades on both sides with many of the larger lions playfully shouldering or pawing the smaller ones. Several hundred carved lions sit atop the balusters of the Seventeen Arches Bridge in Beijing, perhaps in imitation of those on the Lugou Bridge. Many other bridges have a smaller number, such as the four on the balusters at the top of the Fangsheng Bridge in Zhujiajiao. On the approaches to the Lugou Bridge and Seventeen Arches Bridge, as well as countless others, sits a pair of guardian lions, just as they guard temples and imperial halls.

A veritable menagerie of animal sculptures acting as propitious symbols of strength ornament various bridges. Two weighty elephants, for example, serve as buttresses on the west end of the Lugou Bridge, their foreheads leaning against the final post of each balustrade in support. The bronze ox which gazes beyond the Seventeen Arches Bridge in Beijing's Yihe Yuan or Summer Palace, is likewise a symbol of might. Its back holds imperial calligraphy telling of the subduing of the great flood by Emperor Yu. The functional precursors of this gracious ox were likely the four cast iron oxen, each weighing several tons, used as anchors for a 300-meter-long iron chain bridge across the Huang He at Yongji in Shaanxi. Two of them were excavated from the river bottom in 1989.

Large stone rhinoceroses and hippopotamuses were once placed along embankments as protection against floods and, according to Tang Huancheng, came to serve on bridges as well since they could use their horns to "cleave through and quiet down the waves surged up by water monsters" (1987: 288). A mythical hoofed, chimerical creature, known in Chinese as the *qilin*, is considered a good omen on bridges in that its arrival is said to foretell the appearance of a sage. It is found at the head of some bridges as an invocation for "serenity" and "prosperity." One of its best representations is at the foot of the Seventeen Arches Bridge in the Yihe Yuan, Beijing. Monkeys and rabbits, two of the twelve animals of the Chinese zodiac, are sometimes seen as playful ornamentation.

Bats are common animals carved on and about bridges, just as they are in homes and temples. This is because of the homophonic relationship between the Chinese character *fu*, meaning "good fortune," "blessing," or "luck," and the word for bat, *bianfu*. Unlike in the West, where bats are generally avoided and sometimes seen as inauspicious, in China they are regarded as graceful flying animals. Bats are sometimes depicted upside down, as seen in the wooden ceiling structures of covered bridges, with the meaning that "*fu* has arrived," in the belief that stating something will make it happen. Because bats are often portrayed ornately and gracefully, they are sometimes mistaken for butterflies, and the first syllable of the word for butterfly, *hudie*, is itself a near homonym for *fu*. Throughout southern Fujian, where local dialects

pronounce "tiger" as *fu* (*hu* in standard Chinese), the tiger is commonly used also as an emblem for "good fortune." Bats, butterflies, and tigers are frequently shown in groups of five to represent the five essential components of good fortune or happiness: longevity, wealth, health, love of virtue, and to die a natural death in old age.

The lotus, with its potent and varied Buddhist imagery, and the bamboo, a symbol of modesty and immutability, dominate the plant motifs found carved in relief atop the vertical balusters and on the face of horizontal balustrades of Chinese bridges. That the lotus and bamboo have long been significant elements of the religious and secular arts in China no doubt contributes to their use on bridges as well.

Just as in homes, pavilions, and halls, carpenters and painters added ornate decorative panels within the arcades of bridges. Most auspicious emblems do not stand alone, but instead are incorporated in

Top:
At one end of the Lugou (Reed Gulch) Bridge, a mighty elephant serves to buttress the long line of balustrade panels. Elephants are said to have once roamed throughout northern China.

Above:
Said to be an omen of prosperity, mythical *qilin* are chimerical creatures with the head of a dragon, the antlers of a deer, the hooves of an ox, the tail of a lion, and the scales of a fish. Shiqigong (Seventeen Arches) Bridge, Yihe Yuan, Beijing.

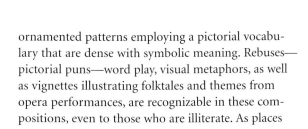

ornamented patterns employing a pictorial vocabulary that are dense with symbolic meaning. Rebuses—pictorial puns—word play, visual metaphors, as well as vignettes illustrating folktales and themes from opera performances, are recognizable in these compositions, even to those who are illiterate. As places to sit and or walk through, China's bridges, like other buildings, provided rich imagery containing easily retrievable and universal messages. While sometimes the motifs incorporating animals and plants are relatively simple, others are part of narrative scenes that express allegorical morality tales.

Red Army Bridges

Red Army bridges—Hongjun Qiao—are found in many provinces in China, with the bulk emerging with that name during Mao Zedong's epic Long March between October 1934 and October 1935. Mao's Long March route involved passage, sometimes in multiple branches, along baffling mountain footpaths and obscure traces through some of China's most difficult terrain, from Jiangxi province in south-central China through portions of Guangdong, Hunan, Guangxi, Guizhou, and Yunnan provinces, before embarking on the longest portion of the route along the rugged ridges of western Sichuan province in southwestern China. Breaking beyond the bounds of the encircling mountains, the troops then crossed less mountainous routes through Gansu province, finally terminating their trek in Yan'an in the tawny loessial plateau of Shaanxi province. Mao claimed that the route was 25,000 *li* or 12,500 kilometers long, an improbably difficult trek to have completed in one twelve-month three-day period, a rousing narrative that subsequently emerged as one of the founding myths of the People's Republic of China.

   Mao's troops, pursued as they were by Nationalist forces, crossed torrential rivers and deep chasms that were often separated by craggy peaks with sheer cliffs, necessitating sometimes the creation of impromptu bridges. Trees could be dropped as makeshift footbridges or small craft tied together to form a pontoon. Some streams could be crossed by fording shallow waters or sometimes a ferry could be used. In some cases, small bamboo or iron suspension bridges provided the only route from one hillside to another, each gaining notoriety in the epic Long March narrative.

Luding Bridge, Sichuan

No bridge along the Long March route has garnered more fame than the Luding Bridge, a Qing-dynasty iron chain suspension bridge, which is slung across the north–south flowing Dadu River that is constrained by steep precipices along both banks. Built in the early eighteenth century, the original Luding Bridge was suspended using thirteen heavy iron chains, nine of which supported a wooden planking deck, while two chains on either side were to be grasped by those crossing the bridge. Since a principal function also was to facilitate the movement of tribute from Lhasa in Tibet to the imperial capital, Beijing, the side chains also thwarted carts and animals from falling off. On both ends of the bridge, the iron chains were anchored into massive stone buttresses, each of which had a building-like structure atop it. The Kangxi emperor visited the bridge in the eighteenth century, leaving behind an inscription; hence its fame also as an "imperial bridge." In 1776, the river rose more than one meter over the bridge, with significant damage to the iron chains. The last great battle of the Taiping Rebellion in the mid-nineteenth century occurred here, with the loss of some 40,000 troops, whose bodies are said to have turned the river crimson for days. Grace Service, an American, wrote in 1908: "The flooring is of irregular

planking with many open spaces. The palings connecting the side chains are few. And there is an airiness about the whole structure hanging so jauntily over the wild and swirling water. The bridge though is vital. One can visualize a thousand varied caravans which have passed over this old trade route. Travelers from India, Nepal, and High Asia have safely crossed the raging Tung by this tenuous cobweb of man's ingenuity. Hidden away in this obscure Chinese valley, it holds the glamor of mystery" (1989: 80). In July 1917, a storm turned the Luding Bridge bottoms up, yet quickly repairs made it serviceable again.

   However significant its pre-twentieth century prominence, the eminence of the Luding Bridge surged as a critical element during Mao's historic Long March when, in late May 1935, a squad of twenty-two soldiers stormed the suspension bridge in what the Communist canon points as a critical assault along the Long March journey. Subsequently, over a seven-day period, perhaps 12,000 peasant soldiers and their leaders were able to cross the raging river and continue to move north to victory. Had the assault failed, Red Army forces might have been wiped out and the revolution aborted. Often-repeated

legend proclaims that the Luding Bridge, which had been stripped of some of its wooden planking to become a mere skeleton, swayed precariously high above the raging Dadu River as the Red Army forces rushed across it while enemy forces on the other side set it afire and lobbed volleys towards them. Huang Zhen, militia leader and subsequent diplomat, immortalized this perilous effort in a contemporaneous sketch, one of only twenty-four drawings surviving that documents the Long March. His view is of a taut span extending from bank to bank high above the water. Later historical images draw attention to the fragmented state of the bridge and the battles that combatants encountered as they surged across, gripping the iron chains as they moved. Today, visitors encounter a reconstructed bridge that offers little that is daunting to those who cross it.

Red and Green Tourism
To commemorate the seventieth anniversary of the Long March, in 2005, China's State Council and the National Tourism Administration designated the year as "The Year of Red Tourism," an initiative designed partially to arouse patriotism and rekindle faith in

the Communist Party, but also to spur economic development via the spending of tourists in backward hinterland areas. Revolutionary sites and specific revolutionary routes were marked and marketed with ambitious efforts to improve infrastructure and entice Chinese tourists to myriad locations of historic interest. While Qinglinkou, Luding, and Qingyuan are hardly equivalent to Yan'an or Shaoshan or Jinggangshan or Shanghai—the best-known Communist revolutionary meccas—they nonetheless are part of the "Red" narrative, and thus are benefiting from increasing tourism. As visitors are able to gain some sense of small town China in remote areas, appreciating their architecture and overall ambience, visitors usually also don Red Army uniforms for personal commemorative photographs as well as enjoy nearby mountain scenery, and perhaps, in the case of Qinglinkou, even take advantage of whitewater rafting on a mountain stream. A promotional jingle for Red Tourism proclaims, "Wear the clothes of the Red Army! Sing the songs of the Red Army! Eat the food of the Red Army! Walk the way of the Red Army!" One tourism official succinctly admitted, "This tourism concept is both Red and Green."

Above left:
This recent painting exaggerates the perils of crossing the impossibly high Luding Bridge.

Top:
A contemporary view of the Luding Bridge reveals its actual height above the Dadu River.

Above:
In the promotion of "Red Tourism" in contemporary China, visitors to the Luding Bridge have an opportunity to dress up in army uniforms and follow a Red Flag across the bridge as part of a re-enactment.

PART THREE

CHINA'S FINE
HERITAGE BRIDGES

BRIDGES OF THE FORBIDDEN CITY

BEIJING

Under a variety of names, the city known today as Beijing served at one time or other over nearly two millennia as the imperial capital for eleven dynasties. As a planned imperial city, its form and character were set in the Yuan dynasty and then further developed during the Ming and Qing dynasties, especially from 1403 to 1911. In the century since, wholesale transformations have substantially reshaped its inherited fabric. Yet, as a comparison of old maps and satellite imagery shows, there remain legible traces of its historic development inscribed throughout its landscapes. While old Beijing is usually described principally in terms of its massive walls and gates—the signatures of imperial authority—it is also important to look at the broader setting of mountains and waterways, which were manipulated to serve both imperial and common needs.

Unlike other major cities worldwide, Beijing was not built astride a river. Indeed, in order to create a road and water transportation network as well as a water supply for the growing city, much effort had to be expended over many centuries to control meandering streams, dredge geometric canals, drain extensive swamps, dig deep wells, and scour open lakes. The construction of the city's encircling walls, moreover, brought with it the excavation of moats, which necessitated a reciprocal relationship that led also to the building of bridges to span the depressions as they filled with water. Throughout the walled city, the canalization of watercourses led itself to the further proliferation of bridges suitable for passage by pedestrians and horse-drawn wheeled carts.

Imperial urban designers, moreover, crafted palace complexes spread over great distances—within and beyond the capital's walls—that became linked together in a system of watercourses along which imperial pleasure barges as well as more practical grain transport and other supply vessels could ply. Traversing the waterways by boat in times past brought enjoyment and contentment to members of the imperial retinue, while sometimes encountering bridges as foils that helped underscore and enhance the distinctive characteristics of scenes as they unfolded along their excursion route. Waterborne travel was not limited to short-term leisure. Over a span of nearly 120 years, the Kangxi and Qianlong emperors made some twelve inspection tours from

Beijing to the Jiangnan region along the Grand Canal. Commemorative scrolls and imperial diaries detailed the bustling scenery along the way, including the significance of the many types of bridges. Within the walled city of Beijing itself, bridges and gates served to modulate hierarchical progressions by the emperor and nobles in terms of their position and height along defined axes. Maps of imperial Beijing in the Ming and Qing dynasties contain countless bridges of varied dimensions that cross moats and canals. While the bridges spanning the city's outer moats are now long gone, one can still see and appreciate the symbolic and pleasurable aspects of some of imperial China's most exquisite bridges within and adjacent to the imperial precincts.

Home to twenty-four emperors for over nearly 500 years, the Purple Forbidden City—named for the Purple Bright Constellation Centering on Polaris, the Pole Star—itself has within it its massive walled precincts a collection of notable bridges, including a set of five in the front as well as smaller ones in the compact labyrinth-like Yuhua Yuan, the Imperial Garden at the rear, and in other wooded areas, with ancient cypress and pines interspersed among the palaces in defined spaces bounded by lesser walls and gates. Like a box enclosed within boxes, the Forbidden City was surrounded by another large enclosure, a set of walls that defined the Imperial City, beyond which was another large area bounded by the actual city walls of Beijing.

Today, one approaches the Imperial City across a set of five slightly raised bridges, each with three openings, that cross the Outer Gold Stream leading to the majestic Tian'an Men or Gate of Heavenly Peace, on which today hangs a striking portrait of Chairman Mao Zedong. An associated pair of outer bridges, some distance away, leads to symmetrical walled areas of great significance for imperial ritual: the tranquil Altar of Land and Grain to the west and the Imperial Ancestral Temple to the east of Tian'an Men. Below the looming gate tower, five of the balustraded marble bridges head towards their own deep portal that pierces the vermillion wall. Today, both areas are public parks with copses of cypress trees, pavilions, paths, and small bridges. Visitors who pass through any of these cavernous gates then emerge into a broad courtyard that spreads before the expansive next entry called Wu Men or Meridian Gate. With 13-meter-high walls and a double-eaved gate tower that reaches nearly 38 meters, Wu Men is also perforated with five gates, through which one actually enters the Forbidden City itself. Here, too, another broad courtyard sets the stage for looking upward towards the Taihe Men, the Gate of Supreme Harmony, which one must mount before viewing the inner sanctum containing the three palace halls that are elevated on terraces.

Between the back of Wu Men and the front of Taihe Men and spanning the courtyard paved with cut stone, a symmetrically concave inward-shaped canalized watercourse called the Inner Gold Stream,

Pages 90–1:
Each of the slightly raised bridges crossing the Outer Gold Stream in front of Tian'an Men or Gate of Heavenly Peace is supported by a larger central arch and two smaller ones. Carved marble balusters separated by prominent posts surmounted by a lotus bud line the deck of the seven bridges.

Above and right:
Across the expansive courtyard in between the back side of the massive Wu Men or Meridian Gate and the imposing Taihe Men, Gate of Supreme Harmony, flows a symmetrical watercourse called the Inner Gold Stream, a companion of the Outer Gold Stream. The Inner Gold Stream is crossed by five parallel white marble single-arch bridges that are often likened to a belt of polished jade.

Top:
Said to be the oldest stone bridge in the palace, having been built at the end of the Yuan dynasty or early in the Ming period, the Duanhong (Broken Rainbow) Bridge once had three arches while today it has only one.

Above:
Paved with thick marble slabs nearly 10 meters wide, the level bridge was modified to look like a completed bridge rather than a rebuilt one.

Above right:
In the Yuhua Yuan or Imperial Garden, a private retreat at the rear of the Forbidden City, there are three rectangular pavilions resting upon marble bridges, which can be viewed as covered bridges.

which mimics those found astride the Outer Gold Stream, is crossed by a parallel set of five white marble single-arch bridges. The curving Inner Gold Stream as well as the bridges themselves are lined with marble balusters, which have been likened to a fine belt of polished jade.

The outer and inner bridges were all built about 1420 during the early Ming dynasty. Each set of five is a duplicate of the other, with the central bridge wider than its neighbors, since it was these bridges that the emperor was carried across, aligned as they—and the associated middle gates—are along the north–south central axis that defined imperial authority. The balusters on these two middle bridges are carved with sinuous *panlong*, dragons said to inhabit the waters and thus represent the emperor. The adjacent bridges, like adjacent gates, were reserved for noble members of the imperial household, while the outer two were restricted to officials above the third grade. Their balusters are capped with a lotus flower. It is said that the five bridges, preserved in their original form, represent the five Confucian cardinal relationships: ruler and subject, father and son, husband and wife, elder and younger brother, and friend and friend.

Above:
One of a pair of *qilin*, a mythical hoofed creature said to bring serenity, which buttress the bridge on both ends.

Right:
The bridge is ornamented with eighteen balustrade panels carved with writhing dragons playing with pearls, as well as carved lions atop square posts.

The confined and narrow Inner Gold Stream is actually a segment of a longer channel whose water is fed from the moat along the northwestern wall. The water then flows due south between the walls of the Forbidden City and the interior walls of the imperial residential quarters, winding through a park-like setting before emerging as the Inner Golden Stream. It then exits again in a meandering path towards the moat on the southeastern city of the complex. In these adjacent poetic gardens of meandering water, geometric paths, and stately trees, are found at least a dozen old marble bridges, including the Duanhong (Broken Rainbow) Bridge, believed to be the oldest stone bridge in the palace. This single hemispheric arched marble bridge is 18.7 meters long, with an especially exquisite balustrade, including eighteen panels carved with writhing dragons playing with pearls. Each of the 1.5-meter-high square posts is capped with a carved lion, large and small, young and old. A pair of *qilin*, a mythical hoofed creature said to bring serenity, buttresses the bridge on both ends. The name "broken" is said to have come about because the actual Duanhong Bridge once had three arches, but that two were removed at some unknown time.

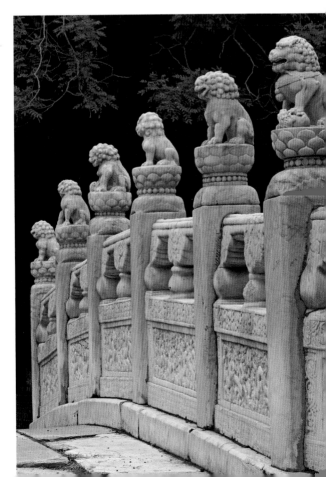

SEA PALACE BRIDGES

BEIJING

Just to the west of the walled Forbidden City and once within the walls of the Imperial City are Beihai, Zhonghai, and Nanhai (North Lake, Center Lake, and South Lake), a triumvirate of interconnected lakes that served as the pleasure locale for Liao, Jin, Yuan, Ming, and Qing emperors. During the Yuan dynasty, the interconnected lakes came to be known as the Pools of Great Secretion, Taiyechi, which then were brought within the Imperial City during the Ming dynasty in 1417 as Xi Yuan, the Western Park. Sometimes referred to as the Sea Palaces, this was an area of informality—in stark contrast to the Forbidden City. It was a somewhat contrived landscape of irregular lakes, waterside palaces, overhanging trees, commanding belvederes, barges in summer and sledges in winter, seasonal flowers and birds, as well as countless serene scenes of pavilions, galleries, halls, stages, and bridges that could be enjoyed throughout the year. A rarely photographed curved bridge reaches to an island called Yingtai or Sea Terrace Island that seems to float on the northern portion of the somewhat circular Nanhai or South Lake. A small bridge called Wugong or Centipede Bridge separated Nanhai and Zhonghai. By the end of the declining Qing dynasty, the Empress Dowager Cixi, who dominated imperial rule for forty-seven years, from 1861 until her death in 1908, came to prefer the solitude of the nearby Sea Palaces in Xi Yuan, arriving by sedan chair after only a ten-minute trip from the Forbidden City. Here, she was able to stroll alone or to host leisurely gatherings that included enjoyment of the many flat, arched, curved, and zigzagged bridges that spanned the complex's narrow channels and embayed areas. The annual cycle of festivals, marked by the progression of lunar months, provided a kaleidoscopic calendar of activities that kept visitors in touch with shifting seasonal vistas at these anchor sites.

Today, the areas surrounding Zhonghai and Nanhai together constitute a new secluded "Forbidden City" known as Zhongnanhai, a precinct appropriated by the State Council of the People's Republic of China

Left:
Viewed from across the Yong'an Bridge, this panoramic view of Qionghua (Jade Flowery) Hill, with the

Yuan-dynasty White Dagoba atop, is today an iconic element of Beihai Park but once was a portion of the secluded Imperial Sea Gardens.

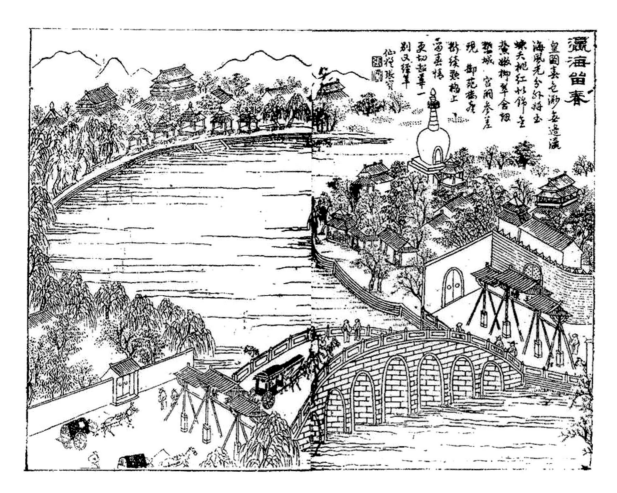

灜海皆春
皇圖表色湖山蓬邁澄
海燕光含外將臺
嫌天桃紅枊翠玉
築嫩枊翠含烟
教城宮開參差
御苑蒼茫
現花御蓮房
新鳞張柳上
更初都里一
蕭叢張柳一
別又簷軍
仙枝張揮

Left:
Struck about 1833, this wood-block print depicts a scene similar to that shown on the previous page, but actually is of a different but nearby bridge, the Jin'aoyudong (Golden Turtle Jade Rainbow) Bridge, a long, low-lying marble bridge separating Zhonghai and Beihai.

Right:
Viewed from the other side, the Yong'an Bridge appears here like its other name, the Wugong (Centipede) Bridge.

and the Chinese Communist Party for offices and residences of many of its leaders. While Zhongnanhai is synonymous with the administration of the People's Republic of China, like 10 Downing Street and the White House, the area is actually made up as much of water as of land and buildings. Sadly, precious little of the imperial era survives in Zhongnanhai in as much as parking areas and functional office buildings have masked the reticulated watercourses, paths, and bridges, leaving only hints of poetically named scenes and structures. Much of this change began in the early years of the republic, beginning in 1912, which accelerated after 1949. Osvald Siren mournfully assessed early changes, saying that they "... have so little to do with architecture as an art that they would be offensive even in a less picturesque milieu" (1949: 111). Beihai, on the other hand, continues to be a tranquil public park that resonates for visitors even today the pleasures of imperial landscapes of times past.

Dividing the waters of Zhonghai and Beihai is Jin'aoyudong (Golden Turtle Jade Rainbow) Bridge, a low-lying massive marble bridge, needed to connect the east side with the west side of Xi Yuan. Built between 1522 and 1566, the bridge was judged by the early twentieth-century sinologist Osvald Siren to be the finest bridge in Beijing (1949: 109), confirming earlier Chinese valorization of the bridge, including that of the Qianlong emperor, who in 1754 wrote a poem to praise the span. The somewhat cumbersome name combines the names of the two *paifang* or memorial archways on each end: the Jade

Rainbow Arch on the east and the Golden Turtle Arch on the west. In order to accommodate modern traffic, the bridge that is seen today was widened in 1958 from 8 meters to 34 meters. During the Cultural Revolution, the marble balustrade was replaced with a purely functional one made of iron, but this was removed in the 1990s. In the past, this bridge and the prominent Lamaist White Dagoba, a rounded pyramidal structure dominated by a spire some 34 meters tall that was built as part of a temple complex atop a hill in 1651, were frequently depicted in woodblock prints. The fact that some woodblock prints show seven arches while others show the nine apparent today reflects a lengthening that occurred early in the twentieth century. For commoners and even foreign visitors at the end of the Qing dynasty, it was possible to walk across this bridge and catch glimpses of the imperial recreational precincts.

Beihai, the North Lake, itself only included two bridges, both providing approaches to Qionghua Islet, atop which is the Yong'an or Eternal Peace Temple. From the south is a low triple-arch structure usually called the Yong'an Bridge since it leads to that temple, but is also called the Wugong (Centipede) Bridge and the Jicui'duiyun (Accumulated Emerald and Piled-up Clouds) Bridge, which reflects the colorful names of the stately four-column wooden *paifang* on each end. Within this tiered precinct, around the lake, are pavilions, halls, towers, galleries, gates, grottoes, inscribed tablets, and ancient gnarled trees. From the east, a lesser bridge runs from the shore to the islet.

Above:
Carved atop each of the pillars is a closed lotus bud, a symbol of purity associated with Buddhist beliefs.

The archipelago-like lakes strewn along the western part of the Imperial City were linked in the north via a water gate to another series of composite lakes, just beyond the walls, called Shichahai or the Lakes of Myriad Monasteries. Shichahai actually includes three distinct lakes: Qianhai or Front Lake, Hou Hai or Back Lake, and Xihai or Western Lake, also called Jishuitan or Pool of Gathered Waters. The historical terminus of the Grand Canal that ran northward some 1800 kilometers from Hangzhou to Beijing, Shichahai was once a bustling commercial area of wharfs and dockside warehouses until its fortunes turned during the Ming dynasty as a result of siltation. Its subsequent development as an area for residential garden complexes for noble Manchu families, most notably Prince Gong, the brother of the eighth emperor Xianfeng who reigned from 1851 to 1861, led to the building of esplanades and linking bridges to take advantage of the planned watercourses and vegetation. The notable bridges include those that divide the three lakes: the Yinding or Silver Ingot Bridge, a Ming Dynasty bridge named for its shape, which is said to resemble a silver ingot turned upside down; the Wanning (Eternal Peace) Bridge; and the Jinding (Gold Ingot) Bridge.

The water system of Beijing drew not only from wells and canals for drinking water but also comprised a network of canalized streams. Although generally perceived as a "dry" city of dusty lanes and high tawny walls, Beijing historically was also a city that was threaded through by a constructed system of waterways that served the needs of commercial

and recreational transport. Sadly, virtually all of the small functional bridges that were necessary components of this system have disappeared. Fortunately, most of the grand bridges built under imperial patronage within the walls of Beijing remain. For the most part, these residual bridges are found in what appear today to be isolated parks, little appreciated for being components of a broader articulated water system of the imperial past that even reached beyond the walls.

Above:
On the north side of Beihai Park, a short bridge leads from the esplanade to a side entrance.

"GARDEN OF GARDENS" BRIDGES

BEIJING

As remarkable as the fine bridges within Beijing's walled palaces are, even more extensive ones are found in the Wan Yuan zhi Yuan or "Garden of Gardens"—literally "10,000 gardens garden"—in the northwestern suburbs some 10 kilometers away from the Forbidden City. At the outset, it is important to recognize that these were not mere gardens for leisure and pleasure. Indeed, throughout most of the Qing dynasty, the Manchu rulers chose to live and administer their empire from these capacious garden-palaces and from their mountain retreat at Jehe rather than from what they viewed as the confinement of the walls-within-walls of the Forbidden City. Designed and expanded throughout the Ming and Qing dynasties, incorporating other earlier gardens as they grew, the rural imperial gardens, known collectively as Yuanming Yuan or Garden of Perfect Brightness, reflected increasing affluence as well as changing tastes. The original Qing-period section was completed in 1744, then added to in 1749 by a section called Changchun Yuan or Garden of Eternal Spring, before being expanded again in 1772 with the inclusion of Qichun Yuan, the Garden of Blossoming Spring, then Qinghua Yuan, the Garden of Pure Flowers, and Jinchun Yuan, the Garden of Arriving Spring, as well as other minor gardens. Many aesthetes believed this complex of magnificent gardens surpassed the ambitious Genyue Park built by the Song emperor Huizong in Kaifeng, which had previously been considered the greatest imperial garden.

The lakes and waterways associated with the Forbidden City and Western Park were linked with the multifarious "Garden of Gardens" complex by a protected canal route along which imperial pleasure barges could move large retinues of courtiers and eunuchs as an alternative to traveling by road in a carried palanquin borne by eight men. Ultimately covering an area of more than 3.5 square kilometers (extensive sections today are incorporated within the campuses of Beijing University and Qinghua University), the gardens were dominated by extensive

Right:
Cast in bronze in 1755, a reclining ox is found at the eastern end of the Shiqigong (Seventeen Arches) Bridge in the Yihe Yuan. On its flank is the carved calligraphy of the Qianlong emperor narrating how the ancient and venerable Sage Emperor Yu calmed floods by controlling the course of rivers.

waterworks and hills, ponds and canals, a variegated terrain of great plasticity. Taken together, these provided exquisite and varying settings for pavilions, palaces, galleries, terraces, arbors, belvederes, archways, retreats, libraries, residences, courtyards, stages, shrines, islets, promontories, temples, studios, pagodas, boats and sleds, in addition to fragrant and flowerful vegetation as well as fish and birds. Bridges and pathways of many types and scales helped integrate the scenic spots of the complex—an ongoing, vast, and imaginative transformation of the cultural landscape that gave many the impression of continuing forever. Cultural and historical treasures—jewels, porcelain, paintings, calligraphy, furniture, religious statues, curios, a vast library, among many others—

that had been handed down from dynasty to dynasty were displayed and stored in structures throughout the gardens. All the buildings and places were draped with allusive poetic names. An inspired addition by Qianlong, who worked with Jesuit missionaries, was Xiyang Lou, a 26-hectare assemblage of palatial buildings, gateways, and fountains—European, primarily Baroque, in style—as part of the Changchun Yuan. In addition, as a result of his many southern inspection tours to places like Suzhou, Yangzhou, and Hangzhou, Qianlong returned with "borrowed" ideas for integrating new garden elements.

While the "Garden of Gardens" flourished in the eighteenth century during the golden reigns of the Kangxi and Qianlong emperors, areas and buildings

began to show lack of maintenance by the early nineteenth century. Tragically, in 1860, and then again in 1900, foreign military forces maliciously ransacked and recklessly smashed its buildings and grounds before setting fires that utterly consumed much of it in a vast conflagration. The sacking—essentially a wholesale destruction—of the Yuanming Yuan in 1860 was the culmination of a joint British-French force that set out to vindictively punish the Xianfeng emperor over perceived indifference regarding treaty obligations, as well as anger over the treatment of European military prisoners. Extensive pilfering by local villagers of minor decorative objects and vast quantities of building materials—cut stone, bricks, roof tiles, wooden columns, doors, windows—to

build their own houses, consequently compounded the devastation. While tentative efforts were made from time to time to restore portions of the expansive complex, diminished financial resources and wavering among those making decisions repeatedly frustrated a comprehensive effort. The one exception was the successful restoration of the imperial locale known today, erroneously, in English by the name Summer Palace which, of course, is the Yihe Yuan, the only fully surviving imperial garden in Beijing's suburbs.

The Yihe Yuan or Garden of Nurtured Harmony was, in fact, a late nineteenth-century "new" garden reborn on the less-damaged Qingyi Yuan or Garden of Clear Ripples, which had been originally built between 1750 and 1764 by the Qianlong emperor to

honor his mother. Since it had not been as seriously marred by the foreign depredation of 1860 as had other nearby gardens, it attracted the attention of the Empress Dowager Cixi, who saw to its renovation during the years leading up to her fiftieth birthday in 1888. For her sixtieth birthday in 1895, she was granted ten million taels of silver, which she then used to complete the Yihe Yuan, including building the fabled Marble Boat. In 1900, what repairs had been made to the imperial gardens, including the Yihe Yuan, suffered a second disastrous blow when an eight-nation force made up of soldiers from Austria-Hungary, France, Germany, Italy, Japan, Russia, the United Kingdom, and the United States entered Beijing to suppress the anti-foreign Boxer Uprising, which had cost the lives of foreign missionaries and countless Chinese Christians. As in 1860, plundering and sheer destruction not only occurred in the newly restored portions of the "Garden of Gardens" but throughout Beijing and Tianjin. With "unbounded extravagance and opulence," as described in the official records, Cixi was undeterred, setting out to do the necessary reconstruction. It was here in the disorder of tarnished splendor that Cixi chose to live out her days during the waning decades of the Qing dynasty until her death in 1908. After the 1911 fall of the Qing

dynasty, the last emperor, Pu'yi, was granted Yihe Yuan as his private property, even as he continued to live in secluded quarters of the Forbidden City.

In the following decade, as the imperial dynasty ended and a new government was frustrated in its formation, general social disorder, inattention, as well as complicit granting of requests to move stone, bricks, wood, and earth, the Yuanming Yuan gardens were further scavenged of what considerable building materials remained. Fragments of artifacts that had survived earlier depredation were gathered up and scattered to places far beyond the gardens. Moreover, the poverty of nearby peasants dealt a near final blow as they transformed the gardens into farmland by flattening hills and filling ponds. The Great Proletarian Cultural Revolution after 1966 then exacerbated the crisis as ancient trees were cut down for fuel, hills were leveled, and remnant stones and bricks were carted off. Except for the Yihe Yuan, which had miraculously endured as it was opened as a public park in 1924, the "Garden of Gardens"—the once sprawling Yuanming Yuan—essentially ceased to exist except in memory, becoming instead a disfigured wasteland landscape devoid of its sublime meanings.

It has only been over the past thirty years that the assaults against the gardens have ceased and

Above:
Using funds said to have been appropriated for the Imperial Navy, the Empress Dowager Cixi restored an earlier structure known as the Boat of Purity and Ease by building a Marble Boat adjacent to the shore of Kunming Lake to celebrate her sixtieth birthday.

contentious discussions set in motion about what level of restoration should be done. Until 2000, fragmentary areas of the landscape were merely tidied up, partially repaired, and sometimes "developed" in ways that did not reflect at all the inherited garden heritage. It is rather a paradox that the most visible relics extant through all of these changes are the eighteenth-century Western-style stone structures, a bittersweet and anomalous reminder of the interplay of cultural accommodation and conflict.

Contemporary Western visitors to the "Yuanming Yuan Ruins Park" often mistakenly assume that the gardens just included European-style buildings, puzzled not only as to why they were constructed but also mystified as to why they were destroyed. Chinese visitors, on the other hand, recall quickly the patriotic messages taught them about the association between the monumental ruins and their century of humiliation at the hands of European "barbarians."

In recent years, sometimes rancorous controversies centering on how to "preserve" the site have consumed bureaucrats, specialists, and the public, with little consensus emerging, even as surveys and plans of various types were carried out. However, in 2000, with the beginning of the new century, the Beijing municipal government committed itself to a course

Top:
These ruins are some of the dramatic stone elements once found in the 26-hectare area known as Xiyang Lou, a cluster of impressive structures built in a European fashion under the direction of Jesuit missionaries during the reign of the Qianlong emperor.

Above:
As the restored centerpiece of a *huanghuazhen*, a labyrinth or maze, designed by Jesuits in the eighteenth century, is this Western-style pavilion.

of perhaps a hundred once found in Yuanming Yuan: "Over the running Streams there are Bridges, at proper Distances, to make the more easy Communication from one Place to another. These are most commonly either of Brick of Free-stone, and sometimes of Wood; but are all raised high enough for the Boats to pass conveniently under them. They are fenced with Balisters finely wrought, and adorned with Works in Relievo; but all of them varied from one another, both in their Ornaments, and Design.

Do not imagine to yourself, that these Bridges run on, like ours, in strait Lines: on the contrary, they generally wind about and serpentize to such a Degree, that some of them, which, if they went on regularly, would be no more than 30 or 40 Foot long, turn so often and so much as to make their whole Length 100 or 200 Foot. You see some of them which, (either in the Midst, or at their Ends,) have little Pavilions for People to rest themselves in; supported sometimes by Four, sometimes by Eight, and sometimes by Sixteen Columns. They are usually on such of the Bridges, as afford the most engaging Prospects. At the Ends of other of the Bridges there are triumphal Arches, either of Wood, or white Marble; form'd in a very pretty Manner, but very different from any thing that I have ever seen in Europe" (1752: 14–15).

While woodblock prints, copper etchings, and nineteenth-century photographs illustrate a variety of small bridges in scenes within Yuanming Yuan, few survived the devastating cataclysm of military action or the quieter predation of poor villagers and ardent collectors in the hundred years after 1860. While wooden bridges might have been consumed in the inferno of 1860, most of the stone plank and stone arch bridges likely succumbed to dismantling by local villagers in search of utilitarian building materials or met the fancy of educated individuals interested in stone sculpture. In 1922, Osvald Siren photographed a triple-opening arched bridge over a mud-filled canal reminiscent of heavy types found elsewhere in northern China. Although apparently still relatively intact at the time, the large bridge somehow vanished in the years that followed. Today, one reads a sign that claims that the adjacent incompletely restored arched span is the "only" remaining original bridge in the garden. Yet, here and there one can also see incomplete bridges composed of old parts, which

Top:
With essentially all the stone components found, this highly ornamented bridge has been reassembled.

Above left:
Held together by metal keys, one ring of this old bridge has been restored.

Above right:
Fractured into several parts, this is one of hundreds of fragments of carved stone strewn throughout the Yuanming Yuan.

Right:
Photographed in the 1920s by Osvald Siren, this multiple arch bridge obviously survived the depredations by foreigners in 1860 and 1900. Its subsequent disappearance is likely the result of villagers removing bricks for their own use in the decades that followed. There is no record of when the bridge vanished.

of "restoration" whose physical manifestation is now emerging in the landscape with surprising speed. In most respects, the Yuanming Yuan is being fashioned into a vast memorial park or garden of elegiac ruins that serve as a reminder of China's humiliation at the hands of foreigners, softened by the reclamation of water-filled lakes and waterways, the planting of trees, shrubs, and flowers, as well as the complete or partial reconstruction of selected representative buildings. Sadly, none of this yet seems capable of capturing the essence of what the gardens once were.

Bridges in the Garden of Gardens

In the Yuanming Yuan and its adjacent gardens, bridges were generally small, yet relatively numerous, and have all but disappeared. In the Yihe Yuan, on the other hand, which had benefited from the ongoing attention of Empress Dowager Cixi, the larger spectacular bridges dating from the eighteenth century peculiarly suffered little damage. Today, the Yihe Yuan bridges are classed among some of the most beautiful in China.

Jean-Denis Attiret, an eighteenth-century French priest, has left the most complete description of the bridges he observed, clearly a subset

Above:
Although incomplete, this high arched bridge is representative of the extraordinary efforts made to reconstruct old structures from stone fragments collected around the site.

Right:
This painting of a bridge that no longer exists in the Yuanming Yuan is part of an exhibition that underscores the great loss of cultural relics over the past century and a half.

are sometimes supplemented with newer replacements. It is likely that the cataloging and stockpiling of seemingly unconnected pieces is making it possible to piece together, like a puzzle, various fragments of bridges into partial wholes.

The standing bridges in the Yihe Yuan, on the other hand, are truly magnificent. There is no large bridge in China with a more beautiful setting than the Shiqigong (Seventeen Arches) Bridge. Moreover, the collection of bridges built under the patronage of the Qianlong emperor along a narrow linear causeway on the west side of Kunming Lake capture what were clearly for him some of the irresistible iconic scenes visited during his southern expeditions to the Jiangnan region.

The Seventeen Arches Bridge, with a length of 150 meters and width of 8 meters, spans a narrow channel between the eastern shore of Kunming Lake and Nanhu Isle in the southeastern portion of the Yihe Yuan. The bridge, built sometime during the Kangxi period between 1161 and 1722, is a monumental structure with arched openings that rise slowly to a crescendo before diminishing, reposing, some say, like a symmetrical rainbow joining the

shore of the lake with the island. When counting the arches from either end of the bridge, from lowest to highest, the count is "nine," an auspicious number since it is the square of "three," another auspicious number. Both numbers are potent *yang* symbols appropriate for the emperor. Along the carved white marble balusters lining the bridge, there are 124 baluster posts, each of which has a carved ornamental lion figure on top of it, perhaps in imitation of the repetitive motif found at the celebrated Lugou Bridge. Altogether, there are some 540 representations of lions on the bridge.

At the eastern end of the bridge, near an octagonal pavilion, rests a bronze ox, cast in 1755, upon which Qianlong's incised calligraphy tells how the Sage Emperor Yu calmed the floods by controlling the course of rivers. The Seventeen Arches Bridge leads appropriately then to the Temple of the Dragon King, the mythical master of water, inside another structure called the Temple of Beneficial and Blessed Rain. The Empress Dowager Cixi is said to have come here regularly to burn incense and pray for rain.

Tucked into a northeastern corner of the Yihe Yuan, behind a small hill which somewhat hides it,

Below:
Viewed from almost the same position as the 1897 photograph on the right, this early twenty-first century photograph shows the extraordinary elegance of the Shiqigong (Seventeen Arches) Bridge.

Right:
Published in 1897 as the Qing dynasty was in decline, this photograph does not obscure the magnificent beauty of the Seventeen Arches Bridge, even as it reveals the inattention to maintenance of the area surrounding the bridge at the time.

is a garden within a garden, Xiequ Yuan, the Garden of Harmonious Pleasures. Constructed to evoke the charm of the Garden of Ease in Wuxi without copying it exactly, the halls, pavilions, terraces, and connecting covered walkways surrounding the small central pond were built on a more reduced scale than those found elsewhere in Yihe Yuan. Most of the architectural features of this southern-style garden are nonetheless more northern than southern in the solidity of their overall appearance. The Knowing

Fish Bridge, with massive stone piers, spans an embayed area in the northeastern part of the garden. Those who cross it easily recollect the amusing dialogue between the philosophers Zhuangzi and Huizi about whether fish know happiness.

Along a 2.5-kilometer-long earthen embankment planted with willows and peach trees—symbols of spring and longevity—are six varied bridges displayed in imitation of those along the Su Causeway on the western side of West Lake in Hangzhou. As they

Above:
With the Western Hills in the distance and Kunming Lake in the foreground, this scene focuses on the horizontal tree-lined causeway and several structures, including the Jade Belt Bridge and the glazed Jade Springs Pagoda atop a ridge called Xiangshan (Fragrant Hills), once an imperial retreat but today a public park.

punctuate the elongated causeway separating a back canal from the body of Kunming Lake, each of the bridges can be appreciated on foot or from a boat as they are approached. All of the bridges enjoy a name inspired by poetry: the Yudai (Jade Belt) Bridge, Jiehu (Lake Boundary) Bridge, Jing (Mirror) Bridge, Lian (White Silk) Bridge, Liao (Willow) Bridge, and the esoterically named Binfeng (Pastoral Poems) Bridge. Except for the Jade Belt Bridge and Jiehu Bridge, the others have a covered pavilion, called a *langting*, atop

Left:
When viewed from a distance, the Yudai (Jade Belt) Bridge appears to rise rather gently. However, when a pedestrian mounts it, the incline indeed is quite steep, as can be seen also on the following pages.

Photographed a hundred years apart, 1906 and 2006, the elegant humpbacked Yudai or Jade Belt Bridge was built of white marble in 1750 and restored at the end of the nineteenth century. Its reflection in the water beneath is like a shimmering full moon.

them with benches on which to rest and take in the view. Each *langting* is capped with a variegated roof and ornamented with paintings on the interior beams. The bridges are sited to "borrow" scenes from the surrounding hills, especially those to the west, and the capacious sky above that is mirrored in the water.

Especially noteworthy is the elegant marble Yudai (Jade Belt) Bridge, which was built in 1750

and restored at the end of the nineteenth century. The only arched structure of the six, it is hump-backed and constructed to rise high like a breaking wave to a height greater than that needed either to facilitate the passage of an imperial barge or ease the ambling of pedestrians along the causeway. With its steep approaches, it is climbed like a precipitously placed ladder. From the top of the double-centered arch, one can enjoy a panoramic scene that includes the Jade Springs Pagoda and the temple-studded Western Hills. The reflection of the bridge in the water beneath is reminiscent of a shimmering full moon. White marble and granite were used to build the bridge's thin shell as well as the balustrades that are carved with designs of cranes in flight on their capitals. When the emperor and empress went by boat to the Jade Spring area in the Western Hills, they passed through the Jade Belt Bridge.

The Bridge of Pastoral Poems or Binfeng Bridge is a lavishly ornamented rectangular covered pavilion that sits atop a hewn-stone bridge with a pair of arcu-ate and one nearly square opening. With its vermil-lion columns, blue beams, and detailed paintings, the bridge is reminiscent of sections of the Long Corridor on the north side of the lake. The bridge predated the building of the Yihe Yuan, having been built earli-er in the Qing dynasty when the garden was known as the Garden of Clear Ripples. Over time, its name

Left and below:
Said to rise high like a wave, the Jade Belt Bridge is mounted as if it were a ladder, leading to a double centered arch where one can tarry to enjoy a panoramic scene of the surrounding Kunming Lake, the Jade Springs Pagoda, and the temple-studded Western Hills.

was changed several times, the final time because the name was homophonous with that of the Xianfeng emperor, which was a taboo. "Bian," an odd character in the name, references a folksong in the *Book of Songs* that celebrated the life of peasants, and was selected, it is said, to call attention to the emperor's concern for agriculture and the peasants.

Chinese gardens, whether private or imperial, are truly environmental art. Like a scroll painting, a garden—whatever its size and however many its components—is to be experienced gradually as a series of scenes are revealed as one passes through it on foot or by boat. Like calligraphy, gardens share common elements while being very individual. Like poetry, gardens are replete with literary and historical allusions. Like architecture, gardens have a three-dimensional form and structure. Gardens are objects that are to be appreciated aesthetically, emotionally, physically, and intellectually. Yet, unlike any other of the Chinese arts, a garden provides more than a visual experience, appealing as well to the sense of sound, touch, and smell. The "Garden of Gardens," in particular, remains today a palimpsest that reflects its competing temporal and spatial manifestations. Bridges, like other contrived spots in the "Garden of Gardens," continue to serve as vehicles to contemplate both the meaning of history and geography as well as the significance of grandeur and decay.

Above:
The Jiehu (Lake Dividing) Bridge, so-named because it divided the inner and outer lakes, was built during the reign of the Qianlong emperor. The bridge once had a pavilion atop it, but it was burned by the Anglo-French forces in 1860.

Right:
Each of the bridges along the back causeway on the west side of Kunming Lake is distinctive. This single-arch span appears like those found in the Jiangnan region.

Opposite:
The Binfeng (Pastoral Poems) Bridge was originally named the Mulberry and Ramie Bridge when the Yihe Yuan was still the Garden of Clear Ripples. With its rectangular shape and double-tiered roof, it is reminiscent of bridges found in Hangzhou.

LUGOU BRIDGE

WANPING, BEIJING

Few Chinese bridges enjoy the worldwide name recognition that the Lugou (Reed Gulch) Bridge has. The Lugou Bridge—known in English as the Marco Polo Bridge—was constructed in a short period between 1189 and 1192 during the Jin dynasty. The bridge is well known by Chinese because it has been celebrated by writers and painters as one of the eight famous sites of Yanshan, the poetic name for the imperial capital Beijing. Near the bridge, a stone tablet with the four graceful characters *Lugou xiao yue* or "The Moon over the Lugou Bridge at dawn," in the calligraphy of the Qianlong emperor affirms the artistic significance of the bridge and its site. Described by Marco Polo in 1280 as "perhaps unequalled by any other in the world," the 266.5-metre-long span, including its approaches, subsequently gained fame in the West as the Marco Polo Bridge. In 1960, the Lugou Bridge was included in the first batch of historic structures to be proclaimed national monuments.

Moreover, Chinese almost universally know of the Lugou Qiao Shibian (Lugou Bridge Incident), what is known in English as the Marco Polo Bridge Incident, considered the first battle of the Second Sino-Japanese War, which lasted from 1937 to 1945, and subsequently led to World War II in December 1941. Taking positions on both ends of this historical bridge, Japanese imperial forces and those of the Nationalist government clashed in a skirmish that unleashed a protracted struggle between the two nations. It was the bridge's strategic chokepoint location straddling the Yongding River, not far from a rail junction line, that brought Japanese forces to the site. As the gateway to the North China Plain, securing the bridge facilitated Japanese efforts to gain control of both large cities and the productive countryside surrounding them.

In terms of construction and ornamentation, the Lugou Bridge has a well-deserved reputation. With a length of 266.5 meters and a width of 9.3 meters, it is the longest multiarched bridge in North China. The eleven semicircular arches vary in size, with those closest to the riverbank being only 11.4 meters wide,

Left:
The massive piers of the low-lying Lugou (Reed Gulch) Bridge serve to deflect floating ice during early spring. The eleven arches marching across the river vary in diameter from 12.35 meters near the banks to 13.42 meters at the center. The profiles of many of the 485 stone lions are apparent in this view.

while the broadest opening at 21.6 meters is in the center where the water flow is greatest. The clear span of the arches increases from 12.35 meters near the shore to 13.42 meters at the center.

Constructed near the walled town of Wanping in Fengtai, a rural suburb about 15 kilometers southwest of Beijing, the design of the bridge responded not only to a need to facilitate north–south wheeled transport but also to address peculiar geographic circumstances that would make vulnerable any structure spanning the river. Bridge builders had to especially address the fact that the shallow Yongding River, which is one of the tributary streams of the Hai River system, freezes over during the bitterly cold winters of northern China. Moreover, it was imperative to have a design that would break up ice floes, thus easing the passage of massive blocks of ice carried from upstream sources during early spring. To address these concerns, multiple arch openings as well as massive boat-shaped cutwater piers helped draw water through and/or deflect and break up the ice as it passed through the arches. Each of the prow-shaped piers, called *fenshuijian* or "points to divide the water," is over 5 meters long, accounting for some 40 percent of the total length of each pier. Triangular cast iron columns were added to reinforce each *fenshuijian* in order to deflect and shear the moving ice.

Like other northern bridges, the Lugou's deck is quite flat in order to facilitate the passage of carts pulled by humans, mules, donkeys, horses, and camels. Accordingly, each of the eleven arches is quite close to

the river's surface, a design made possible because river navigation was not an important factor. Unlike the Zhaozhou Bridge, which has a transverse system of thin wedge-shaped stones to form its arches, the Lugou Bridge employs a longitudinal bond to negate any chance that the arch rings might fall out.

Providing a special character to the bridge are the 485 stone lions that sit atop the capitals along the white marble balustrades lining both sides of the bridge. Around Beijing, a common saying is *Lugou Qiao de shizi, shu buqing* ("The lions of the Lugou Bridge are too numerous to count"), a generalization that arises from the fact that seemingly countless lion statues are carved in a great variety of shapes and are distributed somewhat randomly among the white marble posts. There is some evidence that suggests that the lions on the original Jin dynasty bridge were quite similar and simple. Over time, as replacements were needed during the Ming and Qing dynasties, they became more varied: large and small, stern and playful, looking up or looking down, on one another's head, underfoot, or behind. Some include lion cubs nestling at the feet of a parent or licking his/her face.

Two vividly carved and hefty reclining stone elephants not only guard each end of the bridge, but also are placed as if they are buttressing the upper bridge structure with their weight.

Along the approaches to the bridge there are two stone stelae, one recording the history of the renovation work carried out during the reign of the Kangxi emperor (1662–1722), and the other bearing the

Opposite:
Focusing on the Lugou Bridge, this early Yuan-period painting is said to chronicle the movement of bundled logs on the river as well as stone by land, both of which were necessary in the building of the imperial capital. *Lugou yunfa tu* (Transporting Logs at the Lugou Bridge). © Museum of Chinese History, Beijing.

Above:
This woodblock print shows the Lugou Bridge in 1771 as part of the Qianlong emperor's trip to the Jiangnan region. On the right is a walled portion of Wanping town. Several pavilions are identified, each of which had imperial stelae within them. The river itself is shown surging with abundant flow.

above-mentioned inscription "The moon over the Lugou Bridge at dawn" in the calligraphy of the Qianlong emperor, who in 1751 personally edited the poetic titles for the eight scenic views of Yanjing. Today, the bridge is recognized as a fine location for spectacular views of the moon during the Mid-Autumn Festival, which falls on the fifteenth day of the eighth lunar month, when the moon appears large and especially brilliant. Second only to the Lunar New Year in im-portance to Chinese families, this date is a time to celebrate the harvest by burning incense and lighting lanterns, as well as eating moon cakes. In recent years, while air pollution in North China has often obscured the radiant moon, visitors continued to flock to this and other bridges. During autumn 2006, controversy erupted when a 3-meter-diameter balloon containing two 500-watt bulbs attached to the ground by an electric cord rose above the Lugou Bridge to insure that visitors would see the "moon." However, on that night the sky was so clear that two brilliant orbs—one real and one artificial—shined brightly.

Several major restorations have altered the bridge somewhat, but its foundation and overall appearance remain much as they were when Marco Polo observed its magnificence some 700 years ago. Polo's observation that "ten horsemen can easily ride across it one beside the other" confirms the massive size and stability of the

Above:
Local residents are only able to sell souvenirs on the western approach to the bridge. On the left is one of the imperial stelae that document the rebuilding of the bridge, as well as commentary by emperors.

Left:
Near the bridge are several stone tablets atop a tortoise, one with the four characters *Lugou xiao yue* or "The moon over Lugou at dawn" in the calligraphy of the Qianlong emperor. In the background is a replica of a two-wheeled mule or donkey cart common in the past.

Lugou Bridge. While the low-lying deck was widened and reconstructed with reinforced concrete in the early years after 1949, a parallel modern bridge was also constructed in order to carry increasing amounts of heavy truck traffic. Restoration work accelerated in the 1980s in order to bring the bridge back to its original form. By 1987, stonemasons were busily preparing new balustrades and capitals in anticipation of heightened tourism drawn to the area, and a museum built to commemorate the fiftieth anniversary of the July 7, 1937 Lugou Bridge Incident.

Over the past twenty years, the significance of the bridge as an historic structure that predates Japanese aggression has increased among the public. Soon after 1949, the construction of the upstream Guanting Reservoir, which became one of two major sources of drinking water for residents of the city of Beijing, drew down substantially the water that flowed under the bridge, alleviating in the process the sometimes violent spewing forth of water and ice that historically occurred. Today, the languid and shallow water that rarely fills the streambed seems to belie the circumstances that gave rise to such a substantial and durable structure as the Lugou Bridge. No longer are its approaches a tangled mass of inns and markets with congregating travelers needing to cross the span. Instead, the bridge is now open only to foot traffic within a park-like setting, a fact that helps heighten opportunities to appreciate its structural sophistication and ornamental craftsmanship that were not always possible during its eventful past when traffic to and across the bridge was heavy.

Above:
Nearly 500 carved stone lions in a variety of poses sit atop the columns along the white marble balustrades lining both sides of the bridge.

Below:
Close-up view of the protruding cutwater piers whose purpose was to force ice and water to pass through the broad openings.

ZHAOZHOU BRIDGE

ZAOXIAN, HEBEI

Begun at the end of the sixth century and completed in 605 during the Sui dynasty, the astonishingly elegant and structurally sophisticated Zhaozhou Bridge is the world's first segmental stone arch span. Its audacious structural form—a segment of a circle rather than a semicircle—anticipated similar developments in the West by 700 years, the most notable example being the triple-arch Ponte Vecchio Bridge built over the Arno River in Florence, Italy, in 1345. Moreover, the additional innovation of two openings in each of the spandrels at both ends of the Zhaozhou Bridge did not appear in Western bridges until the nineteenth century. Open spandrel reinforced concrete bridges then became the quintessentially ubiquitous "modern" form throughout the world during the twentieth century. Because of these remarkable early technical innovations, historians of science and technology rank the Zhaozhou Bridge as one of China's principal contributions to world architecture and engineering.

Beginning in 581, during the short-lived Sui dynasty, Chinese imperial control was reasserted over the competing satraps who had controlled the various regions of the country since the decline of the Han dynasty in the third century. Immense public works projects were carried out, including the excavation of the 2400-kilometer-long Grand Canal, the rebuilding of two grand imperial capitals, and major improvements to the Great Wall.

On a more practical level, the long-distance transport of goods and men was critical to the economic viability of the ruling house. The movement of goods by land south and southwest from the North China Plain to the Central Plains around Kaifeng and Luoyang ran along a route that had to cross the Xiao River near Luanzhou (later Zhaozhou and now Zhaoxian) in today's Hebei province. Flowing west to east through a plain that was relatively low-lying on both sides, the Xiao River was an important artery for water transport but an impediment to continuous overland movement and the economic integration of China's regions.

Left:
With two pairs of symmetrical open spandrels, the low-lying segmental Zhaozhou Bridge appears like a modern bridge even though it was completed at the beginning of the seventh century.

Chinese history credits the design and building of the Zhaozhou Bridge—also called the Anji (Safe Passage) Bridge and Dashi (Great Stone) Bridge—to an historical figure named Li Chun who directed masons and other craftsmen in its creation. However, no contemporaneous materials recorded the process. It is left to brief notes in later chronicles, and especially to the bridge itself, to reveal the conditions under which Li Chun broke the stereotype of Chinese arches with his unprecedented construction.

As has been demonstrated throughout this book, the use of arches—singly or in multiples—in Chinese bridge building was common before the building of the Zhaozhou Bridge. As elsewhere in the world at the time, arched bridges had all been limited to semi-circular spans or pointed two-centered arches, either standing alone or lined one after the other to reach across a greater gap. However, while there was substantial versatility in how arches alone or in series could be employed, none of the emerging structures could simultaneously meet the seemingly contradictory demands for both a single long span with gentle approaches and one that reached high enough to permit boat traffic. Single semicircular arches, while providing the kind of lofty arcs common in the Jiangnan region, usually required steep approaches that necessitated the addition of broad steps to make foot passage across them possible. Beam bridges, of course, were limited in their height and individual span. A series of arches each with a small diameter was not the answer either because of the difficulty of sinking stone piers within the riverbed. A single semicircular arch reaching from bank to bank and of sufficient height to permit boat traffic would have had to exceed a rise of 20 meters. Additionally, its weight would have been excessive for the soil and rock supporting the abutments at either end. This was the dilemma Li Chun faced.

None of these options was appropriate on the flat North China Plain where mule-, horse-, and human-drawn cart traffic required a fairly level approach. Confronted with the need to span nearly 40 meters with a stone bridge light enough not to overwhelm its supporting abutments, Li Chun advocated a truly revolutionary principal: it was possible to flatten the curve of the arch if one viewed the arc as but a segment of a much larger semicircle. Such a segment of the large arch could spring from its abutments as a gentle arc that would be much more horizontal than was possible with a semicircular arch. A nearly level roadway could then be laid atop this flattened segmental arc in order to tie the banks together, something never before possible with arched bridges.

The Space Between

Li Chun further suggested a novel innovation for the roughly triangular-shaped spandrels, the area between the deck and roadway and the underlying arch at both ends of the bridge. By piercing each spandrel to create "open spandrels," called *changjian* and *kongfu* in Chinese, Li Chun determined that both the deadweight and live load of the bridge would be substantially reduced, a unique device that came to

be duplicated countless times in Chinese bridges built later. This design clearly accentuates the lithe curvature of any bridge. Today, open spandrel segmental bridge structures are so common in the West as well as in China that they appear "modern," leading one to forget that they had their origin in China more than thirteen centuries ago.

Contemporary measurements reveal that the bridge was lightened 15.3 percent, about 500 tons, because of the four open spandrels; the two larger ones have a diameter of about 4 meters while the two smallest are but 2.72 meters. As a result, the pressure on the abutments was reduced, and over time there has been minimal movement in the overall structure. A Tang-dynasty chronicle of the eighth century records that the open spandrels also served "to sweep away the clashing onrush of angry water" at the time of a major flood, a function confirmed during the floods of 1963 when the open spandrels increased the flow-through capacity by nearly 20 percent over solid spandrels. Accomplishing these several technical objectives, the intervening open spandrels simultaneously also differentiate the structural significance of the uplifting arch from the supported load above.

The arches—those of the major span and those within the spandrels—are formed in the Roman way, with separate but adjacent arcs. Viewed from beneath, twenty-eight parallel arches, each comprising forty-three stones called voussoirs, run the length of each ring. These wedge-shaped stone voussoirs, *xuan* in Chinese, have a height of 1.03 meters, a length that varies between 0.7 and 1.09 meters, and a depth of

Below:
Focusing on the pair of innovative open spandrels, this view also shows the overhanging stone wedges and "iron keys" that act to hold the external voussoirs from collapsing.

Right:
Bounded by bountiful carved ornamentation along its edges, the Zhaozhou Bridge is remarkably level, easing the passage of heavily laden horse carts in times past, even though the distance spanned is great.

from 0.2 to 0.4 meters. Together they form a remarkably thin shell, which is deceptively fragile but actually capable of great flexibility. Recent measurements have shown the near precision of Li Chun and his assistants. The full circle, of which the arch is but a segment, has a radius of 27.7 meters along the west side and 27.3 meters along the east side.

Stabilizing the Structure

Li Chun and his assistants employed several measures to stabilize the parallel rows of wedge-shaped voussoirs that make up the underlying parallel arches of the bridge. First, nine reinforcing stone rods, each welded with a cap to pull in the stones, were horizontally pierced through the twenty-eight arches. Second, the voussoirs were then joined to one another by double dovetail-shaped "iron keys" that were sunk into chiseled indentations in the limestone along the outward-facing surfaces of each arch. Third, as a supplementary device to secure the arches beneath, a course of stone slabs 0.33 meters thick was added. Roughly one-third the thickness of the main arch stones, these stone slabs were laid with their "iron keys" perpendicular to those along the sides of the arches. Fourth, along each of the outer arches, six of the exterior stone slabs were cut so as to overhang, forming "stone hooks" to prevent the voussoirs from falling outwards. Fifth, modern measurements reveal

that Li Chun also designed the arch complex with a slight camber so that it would fall slightly in on itself to increase its stability. The combined width of the twenty-eight arches is 9.6 meters on the bottom but only 9 meters along the top surface. Finally, dragons and offspring were carved profusely on the bridge in the belief that they offered still further protection.

Except for the loss of some outer voussoirs, the bridge has remained intact in spite of floods, earthquakes, and heavy traffic. Local lore among the folk in the Zhaozhou area held that some believed that the arch of the bridge continued as a full circle underground. The eminent Chinese architectural historian Liang Sicheng, who first described the bridge in detail in 1934, had indeed expected the foundations to be very deep. However, his excavations, while discounting the folktales, uncovered only five slabs of stone, each stacked in receding layers one atop the other. These formed the only apparent foundations or bridge abutments at both ends. Although Liang did not find anything besides earth beneath these, he still believed that they were not sufficient to "carry the thrust of this disproportionately large arch" and that further large-scale excavations would uncover "the actual status of the foundation."

Recent fieldwork confirmed Liang's initial discoveries, refined his measurements, but was also unable to locate any deeper foundation. The layered stone

Above:
Double-dovetailed "iron keys" as well as overhanging "stone hooks" were used to prevent the stone voussoirs, the stone wedges making up the arches, from falling outwards.

foundation is unexpectedly a rather small one, measuring 1.549 meters thick, 5.4 meters long, and 10 meters wide, only slightly wider than the bridge itself. Soil analysis shows that the foundation sits within the river's embankment directly on homogeneous clay rather than on coarse sand as reported in various historical accounts. The bearing capacities of the clay and the stone foundation have withstood well both horizontal and vertical forces, and they attest to the practical knowledge of Li Chun and his craftsmen. It may well be that the stable and compacted base for the bridge resulted from its being constructed on the site of well-worn wharfs that marked a ferry across the river at this heavily traveled location.

Stone for the bridge was brought from locations more than 30 kilometers away in the hilly areas of western Hebei province, principally Yuanshi and Zanhuang counties. As with so much other weighty construction in northern China, the bulky pieces of stone were usually moved in winter across surfaces made slippery by spreading a layer of water that froze into ice. This transport method required that the bridge be built section by section over an unknown period of time as resources and weather allowed.

The elegance of the bridge's arcuate lines, symmetry, and spandreled arches led a Ming author to describe it as *chuyue chuyun, changhong yinjian* ("a new moon rising above the clouds, a long rainbow drinking from a mountain stream"). Embellishing the geometry of the superstructure are carved balustrades and posts "in the forms of dragons and beasts, winding crouching and interlacing as if alive," according to the eighth-century Tang chronicle. When Liang Sicheng visited the bridge in the 1930s, all of the original carved surfaces were gone, replaced in a few cases by several "new" ones not older than the Ming dynasty (1368–1644). Some fragments of the early balustrades and posts carved in bas-relief were discovered buried in the riverbed during excavations in 1953 and are now collecting dust in a nearby exhibition hall. The parapet, balustrades, and posts have all now been replaced with newly carved ones replicating those of the Sui period.

A monument to engineering acumen, Li Chun's Sui-dynasty Zhaozhou Bridge was hardly an isolated historical phenomenon. Open spandrel segmental bridges, no doubt patterned after the Zhaozhou Bridge, were later built in nearby areas of Hebei

Above:
Carved into the central stone panel on each side of the bridge is a grimacing *taotie*, an offspring of the dragon. The abutting vertical posts and adjacent panels reveal a variety of facing dragon imagery with sets arranged symmetrically.

Right:
Close-up view of the apex of the central arch showing the copious surface ornamentation, including a keystone carved into the face of a dragon. Double-dovetailed "iron keys" secure the stone wedges from falling outward.

province as well as in other locations in China. Especially noteworthy is the Small Stone Bridge, which is located near by, also called the Yongtong (Eternal Crossing) Bridge, a late twelfth-century reproduction of the Zhaozhou Bridge. Having undergone fewer repairs and rebuilding until recent times, it too has aged gracefully by the minimal shifting of its foundation and the weathering of its stone.

The Chinese regard the Zhaozhou Bridge as one of the country's outstanding achievements, a monument to the high levels of science and technology in imperial China that often preceded innovations in the West. In spite of the deserved pride that the Chinese have shown in the bridge and the notice it has received by some Westerners, worldwide acclaim for the Zhaozhou Bridge has been slow to come. In 1989, however, the American Society of Civil Engineers declared the Zhaozhou Bridge an International Historic Civil Engineering Landmark, a recognition that has brought substantial attention to the bridge specifically and civil engineering in China generally. Today, the Zhaozhou Bridge stands within a park-like setting focusing not only on the structure but also on the historical circumstances that gave rise to the

bridge in southern Hebei. New bridges near by carry heavy traffic across them, linking up with the successor roads of those that were originally traced along routes that date well before the seventh century.

DULIN BRIDGE AND SHAN BRIDGE

CANGZHOU, HEBEI

Old bridges of substantial proportions, distinctive design, and rich ornamentation are strikingly widespread in rural and urban China, although relatively few of them are "known" beyond the communities in which they are located. It may not be obvious that most such bridges once were quite important structures locally and many had countrywide fame. Yet, over the course of time, because of the waxing and waning of fortunes as well as inattention and lapses of memory, once-important bridges—as well as other buildings—tend to be "forgotten" until some authority recognizes their provenance and calls attention to them. Not only are so many of them not noticed in China, they never even rise to a level of consciousness, let alone significance, to others beyond China.

An article in 2003 by Lucie Olivová called attention to two such forgotten bridges built in the later

years of the Ming dynasty in southern Hebei province: "Given their four centuries of age, their monumental size, their distinct type of construction and their exuberant decorative sculpture, Dulinqiao and the echoing Shanqiao do not deserve to be forgotten" (p. 232). Moreover, one has to be puzzled by the fact that stone bridges are numerous in a region that does not have stone quarries and where masons are few. Throughout southern Hebei and nearby areas of Shandong province, tamped earth and adobe brick construction are the norm for houses and shops, but neither building material was suitable for bridge construction. Following her lead, we visited both bridges on a hot day in the summer of 2006. We were not disappointed.

The region south of Beijing and Tianjin and to the east of the provincial capital Shijiazhuang, which historically has always been densely populated, is

Below:
Located some 60 kilometers west of the Dulin Bridge, which it resembles, the longer Shan Bridge, at 75.5 meters, was completed in 1640 after a protracted eleven-year period because of difficulties in the waning years of the Ming dynasty.

Right:
It is likely that the panel depicts a scholar's dream. Dulin Bridge.

Below right:
Constructed in 1594 of stone transported some 200 kilometers from the Taihang Mountains, the Dulin Bridge is a substantial bridge 66 meters long spanning the Hutuo River. Today, the riverbed is dry.

geographically like most of the North China Plain, a broad floodplain layered with tawny alluvial soils with few topographic obstacles except for old rivers. Sorghum, millet, and wheat are the traditional crops while New World crops, such as maize, peanuts, and tobacco, gained prominence from the sixteenth century onward. These local crops and commercial long-distance trade helped sustain a growing population in large nucleated villages across what clearly has been one of the most densely populated regions in the world. Both flood and drought historically have afflicted the overall regional watershed, one dominated by the Huang He (Yellow River) as well as the many tributaries of the once-important Hai He. Today, when water flowing in the Huang He is rare and most of the tributaries that feed the Hai He have reverted to being dry riverbeds, it is difficult to imagine a time

when fords, ferries, and bridges as well as boats of different types were critical components of an extensive commercial transportation system.

Olivová asks: "How is it possible that the beautiful, solid stone bridge sprang, as it might seem today, practically out of nowhere, in Dulin?" Besides detailing the climatologic and topographic elements and practical considerations, she translates documentation found on a stele dated 1594 that it was the meritorious deed of an official, Ruan Shangbin, that led to the construction of the bridge: "A change was needed, but there never has been a magnanimous official who would reduce his own property, take over command, gather workers, provide material, and order Taoist monks to collect contributions. Then I arrived and gladly said, 'This would be a propitious and beneficial deed.' I cut my salary to assist the accomplishment of the construction. Thick layers of earth were piled up to sustain [the construction]. The supporting pillars are large, not to be encircled by outstretched arms. Truly solid. If rushing and flowing waters roll over this flat land again, they would cause no more damage. The bridge is protected by a mound from the east. The bridge has five arches, which let the flow pass unhampered. From then on, [the journey on] the imperial road has not irritated the people, and they do not moan in distress. In a twinkling of [an] eye, they can reach [the other bank]. Oh, rejoice, loaded roaders! Were there ever again the ford, would [I] not pay twenty thousand for a certain profit? Besides, ten millions were donated. Opinions are not united: The works took long and were demanding; toll collectors are not happy to have lost the ford. The merit has not come easily'" (2003: 226–7).

A stele 300 years later records additional information revealing that Ruan's effort may have been substantially more self-serving as he held the office of salt commissioner, a lucrative position since the production and distribution of salt was an important imperial monopoly that designated officials could benefit from. The stele directly states that a compelling reason for constructing the bridge was "to make the transport of salt easier."

Unlike the lithe Zhaozhou Bridge, with its pierced spandrels and expansive segmental arch that seems to lift the bridge effortlessly, the Dulin Bridge by contrast appears ponderous and heavy. Constructed in 1594 of copious amounts of stone that had to be transported some 200 kilometers from the Taihang Mountains in

Above:
Seven meters wide and modified in 1913 to allow motor vehicular traffic, today the Dulin Bridge is principally crossed by tractors, carts, motorbikes, and pedestrians.

Far left:
The triangular-shaped cutwaters, which face upstream, served once to deflect ice floes in winter and storm surges at other times.

Left:
This carved balustrade panel narrates a morality tale.

Below left:
Carved above each upstream arch, water dragons called *baxia*, said to be good swimmers, serve more as totems to guard the bridge than as mere ornaments.

western Hebei to Dulin village, the bridge is 66 meters long, 7 meters wide, and stands 9 meters above the riverbed of the Hutuo River. While lacking the simple elegance of the Zhaozhou Bridge, the lines and arcs of the Dulin Bridge nonetheless are pleasingly symmetrically and are finely fashioned. Three arches—two 17.4 meters and one 18.5 meters in diameter—create a surface sufficient to support the 7-meter-wide deck. Two smaller arches set vertically 3.75 meters tall and 3.25 meters wide act to lighten the central pair of spandrels. The height and width of the bridge as well as the accumulated deposition along both its sides suggest that the river sometimes seasonally carried great volumes of water and ice. Indeed, flooding in 1894 caused the collapse of one of the larger as well as one of the smaller arches, impacting the bridge's use for fourteen years until repairs could be completed. By 1913, additional modifications were made to allow motor vehicular traffic. Even today, the bridge meets the needs of villagers with an increasing variety of vehicles.

As with other North China bridges, the Dulin Bridge is embellished with abundant stone ornamentation, including a pair of freestanding lions, statues of animals poised on pillars, and balustrades with relief carvings. Monkey statues, which are not a particularly common architectural motif, especially are numerous. The monkey, pronounced *hou*, is homophonous for the term for official, and thus may symbolize the wish of donors to the bridge for official advancement. Each of the forty-six oblong balustrade slabs is carved, some with simple floral patterns, auspicious animals and plants, landscapes,

and pictorial scenes of morality tales. The images carved on three of the slabs were completely expunged during the Cultural Revolution while others were shattered into fragments. Above the arches are carved masks of water dragons called *baxia* that function more as totems guarding the bridge than as ornaments decorating it.

Crossing the Hutuo River at a location some 60 kilometers west of the Dulin Bridge, which it resembles somewhat although its scale is larger, the Shan Bridge was begun some thirty-five years after the Dulin Bridge and completed in 1640 after an eleven-year period of construction. This long period of construction was attenuated because of the difficulty of raising sufficient capital, a condition perhaps reflecting the overall economic difficulties associated with the final declining years of the once-vigorous Ming dynasty.

Constructed of blocks of cut granite stone, the Shan Bridge has an overall length of 75.5 meters and a relatively flat 9.5-meter-wide deck that rises gently from the flaired approaches. Five semicircular arches with an equal diameter of 9.9 meters are separated from each other by four slightly elevated smaller flow-through arches that lift the decking. While blocks of granite laid horizontally are held together only by gravity, those angled to form arches are secured with symmetrical iron keys. Each of the vertical and horizontal stone components making up the balustrade are connected by mortar-and-tenoned joinery chiseled by the stonemasons in a fashion replicating that of carpentry. Modular construction of this sort not only eases onsite construction at the

Below:
As with other arch bridges made of stone, the components are carefully cut as replicable modular pieces.

beginning but also facilitates replacing parts of the bridge as needs demand with the passage of time.

At one point, the surface of the bridge must have been quite level, with each of the granite pavers lodged closely with its neighbors. Over the years, however, the stones comprising the pavement weathered unevenly so that the bridge's surface became for the most part uneven and corrugated. Periodic maintenance with earth and stone fragments used to infill particularly uneven sections was necessary. From time to time, whole sections would be replaced. Today, two-thirds of the width retains the rugged texture of centuries of wear and tear while the remaining section is relatively flat. While irregularity of the surface forces a pedestrian, even one using a shoulder pole, to walk carefully, crossing the same bumpy surface as a rider on the back of a gingerly stepping mule or horse, on the other hand, it affirmed the truism that "The outside of a horse is indeed good for the inside of a man." Yet, riding in a traditional northern China mule cart was a jarring experience, whether on roads or bridges. A missionary who chanced riding a mule cart in 1901 declared that it was "about the most uncomfortable conveyance that the ingenuity of man has yet devised. The unhappy passenger is hurled against the wooden top and sides and is so jolted and bumped that,

as the small boy said in his composition, 'his heart, lungs, liver, kidneys, stomach, bones and brains are all mixed up'" (Brown, 1904: 55). Mule carts are still widely used in northern China, although today they are likely to be fitted with tires like those found on trucks.

Ornamentation of the Shan Bridge is similar to that of the Dulin Bridge, especially in terms of statues of animals and balustrades carved in low relief, but for the most part they are coarser than those on the earlier bridge, again perhaps because of insufficient funds and the need to make do. While the motifs on the fifty-four stone balustrade slabs lack any unifying theme, they cover a range of topics, including filial piety admonitions and historic morality tales. Many of these also were vandalized during the Cultural Revolution. Nine totem-like dragon *baxia* rest atop the nine arch openings.

In early 2006, the Dulin Bridge was approved as a national-level historic site while the Shan Bridge remains a provincial-level site. Neither is "forgotten" any longer. Thirty-five years ago, in one of his early *Science and Civilization in China* volumes, Needham reminded us: "No ancient country in the world did more in civil engineering, both as to scale and skill, than China, yet very little has been done towards making known the history of it" (1971: 4(3) 1). The

fault is both internal and external. Indeed, those with an interest in Chinese buildings and landscapes who read extensively and travel widely in the country regularly continue to stumble across structures that jar one's sense of what is known about Chinese architecture and culture. One is often forced to ask, how could something this significant and weighty be "lost?" While increasingly many are being "found" and elevated out of obscurity, much work yet must be done to understand the relationships among structures as well as the broader historical, economic, geographical, and iconographic circumstances surrounding their origins and maintenance over the succeeding years.

Right:
Near vertical arches on the Shan Bridge are placed also on the Dulin Bridge above each cutwater and function to heighten water flow-through during periods of heavy flood.

Far right above:
Small carved shrines, each housing a Buddha image, alternate with carvings of animals along the Shan Bridge. It is not clear how they were used by the pious who crossed the bridge.

Far right below:
Alternating with other auspicious animals such as the dragon and lion, a *qilin*, a mythical beast that shares the parts of other animals, sits atop columns on the Shan Bridge.

JINGXING BRIDGE

CANGYAN MOUNTAINS, HEBEI

Temples and temple complexes in China are found in incredible variety. While most urban and rural temples are small and modest, others are extensive walled complexes with halls, pagodas, quarters for monks and devotees, as well as awe-inspiring ancient trees and stones. Throughout the mountains of China, there are secluded Daoist and Buddhist temples built for monks and nuns who favored quiet mountains and deep forests for their meditative practices, thus wanting to retreat from the clamor of secular life in hard-to-access locations. Over time, some of these small hermitages developed into great monastic complexes, especially among the peaks held sacred by Buddhists and Daoists who believed that the variegated landscapes possessed a spiritual force or essence. In some cases, lay practitioners, knowing of these special remote redoubts, came to make arduous pilgrimages to them by climbing countless steps or following steep paths and ledges in order to pay homage to images of Buddhas, Bodhisattvas, as well as other gods. While

some temples, such as the Jinci Temple in Taiyuan, incorporate noteworthy bridges in the spatial layout of their precincts, many more temples have nearby bridges associated with them or, as we have seen, with many covered bridges, an altar for offerings is frequently built within the bridge's structure.

It is a rare temple in which the religious structure itself is actually perched on a bridge, with both existing *only* in relation to the other. Such is the case with Jingxing Bridge and the Qiaolou Hall built atop it that are located in the Cangyan Mountains, about 70 kilometers west of Shijiazhuang, Hebei. This craggy mountainous area is part of the better-known Taihang Mountain range, which straddles the rugged border between Hebei and Shanxi provinces. With peaks that soar some 1000 meters above the plains below, the precipitous landscape is characterized by deep ravines and rock surfaces with often grotesque shapes. Swiftly moving mountain streams, moreover, toss boulders from high areas to those below, creating

Below:
If the two-storey Qiaolou Hall (Bridge Building Hall) had been built on solid ground, it would have been considered a fine structure. Perched atop a soaring arched bridge, it represents an exceptional engineering feat. As shown here, the temple is reached from below via a set of steep stone steps that situate the place of worship along the pathway crossing the bridge, of which it is structurally an integral component.

Right:
Clutched between precipitous cliff faces, the bridge and temple comprise a rare structure whose method of construction is lost in history. In the background is a modern prestressed concrete bridge built to facilitate the movement of increasing numbers of visitors to a site that once was difficult to access.

Left:
The grandeur of the overall site is clearly seen in this view looking back from the ascending path along the cliff face leading to smaller shrines. In the foreground is a modern span that obscures the ancient bridge supporting Qiaolou Hall. To the left is a smaller structure, shown in the photograph above, which houses subsidiary deities.

Above:
Rough stonework has been used to disguise the makeup of the modern bridge on the left, which leads from the secondary temple beyond to a narrow path that devotees must climb to reach countless smaller shrines.

Right center:
Alternating gold and green glazed roof tiles not only cap the main Qiaolou Hall but also many of the large and small ancillary structures.

Right bottom:
Beneath the overhanging eaves are elaborately carved wooden bracket sets and elongated panels between the columns.

great danger to residents and visitors. Anyone contemplating living on its slopes is challenged to find sufficient level land to construct a building.

Qiaolou Hall (Bridge Building Hall) is the main structure of Fuqing Temple, whose extent spreads along the mountain pathways where countless grottoes and small structures serve as individual votive locations for a broad pantheon. The complex is said to have been built at the end of the Sui dynasty or the beginning of the Tang dynasty, during the seventh century. This traditional dating, however, has been contested with opinions that suggest the construction took place some time later, between the eighth and twelfth centuries. While accurate dating is important, the lack of precision does not detract from the fact that this extraordinary bridge-hall structure has been standing, not precariously, but firmly, for more than a thousand years.

Situated on a stone arch bridge that spans a precipitous gap between opposing cliffs, Qiaolou Hall appears to be suspended some 70 meters above the ground below. The bridge-building is reached only after climbing a winding staircase, here called a "heavenly ladder," with some 360 stone steps. In the first instance, the structure is a bridge that allows passage from one mountain stone pathway to another that could only be accessed by a bridge. Secondly, the bridge serves as the level foundation for a two-storey

Far left:
At the terminus of the cliffside trail is a brick furnace used to burn offerings. On the table in front, a women is folding colored paper in the shape of gold ingots that will be sold with incense as offerings to be consumed in the fire.

Above left:
At the base of the mountain adjacent to the main path leading up to Qiaolou Hall is a busy shrine where visitors can make offerings before images of past political leaders like Mao Zedong, Zhou Enlai, and Deng Xiaoping, who to some have achieved a deity-like status.

Left:
The eclectic nature of worship within the mountain precincts is suggested by the sometimes odd proximity of scrolls with images of goddesses, historical figures, and immortals.

Bottom left:
The main deity within Qiaolou Hall is Sakyamuni, the Present Buddha, who is accompanied by the Medicine Buddha and Amitaba, the Future Buddha.

religious building. Together, the bridge and building form an indivisible structural unit.

The underlying bridge structure is reminiscent of the Zhaozhou Bridge, described in detail on pages 122–7, in that the single-arch span is accompanied by a pair of open spandrels in the roughly triangular space between the exterior curve of the arch. Open spandrels of this type lighten the load carried by the arch. Overall, the bridge has a length of 15 meters, a width of 9 meters, and stands at least 70 meters above level ground. The half moon-shaped arch itself has a diameter of 10.7 meters and a structural height of 3.3 meters. The scale and structure of the bridge is reminiscent of ones found elsewhere in Hebei, such as the Guding Bridge in Ningjin county.

The two-storey temple hall is constructed using common wooden components. Eaves columns create a roofed gallery around the structure, which is five bays wide and three bays deep. The double-tiered roof is covered with yellow roof tiles. Inside, there are numerous statues of deities still worshipped by countless breathless pilgrims who make the arduous journey upwards into the mountains to reach the temple's magnificent site. While the two-storey hall has been renovated several times because of deterioration of its wooden components, there are no records of repair of what might seem to be a potentially unstable bridge structure but one that has remained securely lodged between a pair of facing precipices. Film producer Ang Lee utilized the awe-inspiring Cangyan Shan mountainscape, including the immediate environs around the inimitable Jingxing Bridge, for some of the fighting scenes in his award-winning movie *Crouching Tiger, Hidden Dragon*.

Left:
This male lion, with its right paw atop a ball, joins a female companion at the base of a set of steps leading to the mountain temple.

Below left:
With a rounded belly, bald head, and jolly smile, this figure is often referred to as the Laughing Buddha, believed by many to be an incarnation of Maitreya, the Future Buddha. The children on his head and at his feet contribute to symbolizing good fortune, progeny, and happiness.

Right:
This small shrine is wedged into a fissure in the face of the cliff where the flagstone-lined pathway is forced to cross a small bridge.

BALING BRIDGE

WEIYUAN, GANSU

Right:
Sweeping upward above
the water, the graceful arc
of the Baliing Bridge reveals
its underlying structure of
bundled logs embedded
into the opposing stone
abutments that then project
upward, where a level set
of logs completes the gap.

Beautiful bridges are sometimes found in what strikes
even knowledgeable observers as unlikely locations.
Nearly four hours by car to the east of Lanzhou in
the semiarid province of Gansu in northwest China
is Weiyuan, a nondescript out-of-the-way town with
one of China's truly magnificent bridges—the Baling
Bridge, a sweeping wooden structure that epitomizes
the art of bridge craftsmanship built by what Peter
Coyne called "carpenters of the rainbow" (1992: 32).

The expression "rainbow bridge" or *caihong qiao*
is unfortunately used loosely throughout China to
describe a broad range of different types of bridges,
from long flat ones to short humped ones. Yet, in
the Chinese mind, as in the minds of others in the
world, the concept of a true rainbow bridge is a
fantastic iridescent structure that rises precipitously
as a symmetrically concentric arc. Elsewhere is
described the well-known timber arched rainbow
bridge, a fixture of Zhang Zeduan's late eleventh-
century *Qingming shanghe tu* painting, that once
soared from its abutments along the banks of the
Bian River at Kaifeng, Henan province. The large
number of existing rainbow bridges in Zhejiang
and Fujian provinces, also described on pages 218–
47, reveal the continuity and endurance of techniques
and approaches employed by carpenters to overcome
steep and turbulent mountain streams with functional structures of notable beauty. All such rainbow
bridges are remarkable and many express truly
sophisticated methods of timber frame construction.

Yet, the Baling "Rainbow" Bridge stands unique
since it not only spans a relatively flat stream but
because its gracefully rising arc and articulated timber
structure combine technical ingenuity with a refined
aesthetic sensibility. Level bridges had crossed the
Qingyuan River here just outside the South Gate of
the walled city of Weiyuan from 1368 until the early
part of the twentieth century. In 1919, as a result of
some inspired civic boosterism, a decision was made
to build a new wooden bridge on this site that was to
be modeled after a well-known bridge in the provincial capital, Lanzhou.

Called the Wo (Holding) Bridge, the Lanzhou
bridge that inspired the Baling Bridge in time became
better known by the homophonous name Reclining
Bridge because of its steep incline, an appellation
also sometimes applied to the Baling Bridge. Said to

have provided a link on the Silk Road as it crossed the Agan River, the Wo Bridge was likely constructed during the Tang dynasty (618–796) and then restored in 1904. In 1952, because of the widening of a road near the bridge, there was discussion of dismantling what was considered a matchless bridge and reassembling it at a different location. Sadly, because of the discovery of severe rotting of the timbers, substantial overall structural damage, and insufficient resources to restore the bridge adequately, a decision was made to demolish Lanzhou's rainbow bridge. Written records show that the demolished bridge had a span of 22.5 meters and an overall length of 27 meters. The enclosed portion of the covered bridge was 4.85 meters tall and had a width of 4.6 meters. A scaled wooden model was crafted and placed in the Lanzhou Museum as, one might suggest, a minor gesture to keep its memory alive.

Although the source of funds for and details concerning the construction of the Baling Bridge are not clear, the magnitude of its construction suggests that the distinctive bridge was to stand as a civic icon. Spanning 29.4 meters, one-third greater than its Lanzhou antecedent, it has an overall length of 44.5 meters and width of 6.2 meters. Sweeping to a height of 15.4 meters above the stream, the roof of the symmetrical gallery reaches even above the surrounding treetops.

In an area deficient in timber, the bridge stands out in terms of the abundance of large logs used in its underlying structure and the attentive carpentry finishes employed in the construction of the surmounting open-sided structure atop it. Four layers of bundled logs, each layer longer than the one beneath it, were embedded in each of the facing stone abutments. Projecting outwards at an upward symmetrical angle, a total of ten sets of bundled logs reach a high point without touching, leaving a gaping breach that was spanned with a set of bundled beams to compose a sweeping curve that reaches nearly 30 meters. Crossbeams mortised to uprights tied the understructure to the deck, providing increased stability for the bridge. At both ends, additional stone and masonry work not only created a stepped entryway with walls but also afforded needed downward pressure on the abutments below. The heavy yet elegant open-sided wooden arcade, with its bracket sets and upturned tile roof and mortise-and-tenoned joinery, while appearing to be somewhat fragile, is actually quite heavy and exerts considerable downward forces that offset the load on the cantilevered beams. Sixty-four columns lift the roof structure and divide the gallery into thirteen structural *jian* or bays. The covered "building" that sweeps upward along a gentle curve from the brick and tile entryways was given shape beneath by segmental chords that mask whatever jaggedness is inherent in the structure, and serve also to protect the underlying structure from the elements.

Above:
Spanning a shallow stream that floods infrequently, the Baling Bridge nonetheless rises high in a symmetrical arc above any possible danger from rushing water.

Top:
View of the interior gallery of the bridge showng some of the sixty-four rather slim pillars that lift the roof via a simple post-and-beam wooden framework.

Left:
On both sides of the bridge, four layers of bundled logs, each longer than the one beneath it, project upward where they are joined by a layer of horizontal beams laid across the gap. Cross-beams mortised into uprights tie this substructure to the deck above.

Above:
On both ends of the bridge is an entry pavilion with upturned eaves and beams lifted by bracket sets. The heavy side walls of baked bricks contrast with the light wooden structure of the bridge itself.

HONGJUN BRIDGE

QINGLINKOU, SICHUAN

While the Luding Bridge has gained fame as the site of an heroic battle between the Red Army forces and the pursuing forces of Chiang Kai-shek, other Red Army bridges served more mundane, but important, purposes. Along the route, armies sometimes billeted in villages and small towns where, according to local and official lore, property and weapons were confiscated from landlords and warlords, social change was fostered, and poor peasants were recruited. In some towns and villages, old bridges were renamed a "Red Army bridge" to mark their new revolutionary role.

No Red Army bridge in Sichuan is more famous than the one in Qinglinkou, a village some 50 kilometers from Jiangyou city in the northwestern portion of the province. Qinglinkou, which straddles a mountain stream, not only was an important market town for villagers living in the surrounding mountains but it lay on the difficult interprovincial trade route between Chengdu to the south and Xi'an to the north. Towns such as Qinglinkou, here on the lower slopes of the mountains, held periodic markets that provided a place for those living off the mountains to market goods they had collected as well as purchase the limited needs they had. Paths typically connected towns with one another so that peasants could carry goods on shoulder poles or in wheelbarrows to market. Limited level ground meant that shops and stalls lined narrow stone-paved lanes with bridgeheads; indeed, the bridge itself as well as the courtyards of temples, served as locations for stalls as well as places to rest and talk. On non-fair days, towns were usually rather quiet places, while on fair days, steady streams of pedestrians flowed into town. Throughout market towns of this type, numerous teahouses and wineshops served as sites for socializing.

Constructed during the middle of the Qing dynasty and known originally as the Heyi (Combined Benefit) Bridge, the span served as the link between the two halves of the town on both banks of the stream below. Little is known about the construction of the bridge; and it is left to its current form to tease out the facts. The bridge itself is comprised of a solidly built

Right:
Connecting sections of town on both sides of the mountain stream, the former Heyi (Combined Benefit) Bridge was reincarnated as a Red Army Bridge (Hongjun Qiao) after 1935, when it served as a locus for political education for the local population.

Above:
On each of the red stars along the balustrades are two Chinese characters, *ba yi* (Eight One), commemorating the Nanchang Uprising on August 1, 1927, commemorated also as the founding date of the Red Army, which since 1945 has been called the People's Liberation Army.

Right:
Standing beside a carved stone stele proclaiming the slogan "The Red Army is the Savior of Poor People," this elderly blind gentleman says that he remembers when the Red Army was billeted in Qinglinkou.

base of three symmetrical stone arches, a larger one in the center flanked by a pair of smaller ones. While most of the time the stream flowing beneath is languid, it can become a rushing torrent during early spring as it is fed by snow melting in the mountains, and in summer by torrential cloudbursts. Mounted via a series of broad stone steps from the main commercial lane in Qinglinkou, the bridge leads to a second perpendicular lane in front of buildings that runs along the stream to the town's main temple. The massive wooden building atop the bridge was constructed using mortise-and-tenoned joinery, with each column set atop a square stone base. Rising above the roofline is a small garret, at one time a shrine with a deity but today empty.

All of the wooden members are painted red, an obvious commemoration of the bridge's twentieth-century Communist reincarnation as a Red Army icon. In April 1935, the Fourth Regiment of the Red Army established a "soviet" base in Qinglinkou, involving itself in a peasant struggle against landlords and propaganda relating to social change. While the Red Army camped in nearby shops, some of which today have placards stating their use, the army used the bridge as an "auditorium" for popularizing various movements. As foci of these efforts, slogans to inspire action and to warn against certain tendencies were emblazoned on walls and carved on old stone stele

and gravestones. Many of these have been collected on the bridge, where one can read both the 1930s slogans as well as the Qing-dynasty texts beneath. Among the bold slogans in red calligraphy are "The Red Army Is the Savior of the Poor," "Free Marriage," "Support Land Reform," "Participate in the Red Army's Division of Fields," and "Resolutely Oppose Imperialism and Fight the Japanese." Red stars and red flags, carved from stone, sit atop the balustrades.

Although there is no evidence remaining of which deities were once worshipped within the bridge, along a narrow lane there are two nearby active temples, the Huoshen Shrine and the Wenchang Palace. Both of these structures include within them several additional deities other than the dominant Daoist ones: Huoshen, known as the Fire Spirit or Fire God, is worshipped widely in China, as is Imperial Sovereign Wenchang, who is sometimes referred to as the God of Literature.

In general, townspeople and villagers enter small religious facilities such as these as the spirit moves them or when there is a request that needs to be made. Trays of food as well as fragrant incense and lighted tapers are regularly placed before images of the deities, offered usually with a prayer. A woman attendant is ready to help any of the supplicants, especially if there is a request to shake a tube of bamboo slips in pursuit of a prognostication.

Opposite above:
This approach to the Hongjun Bridge passes by shuttered shops, which on market days are opened when villagers arrive in great numbers.

Above:
The view looking out from the middle of the Hongjun Bridge shows the streamside housing, with the characteristic dark wooden members with whitewashed wattle and daub infilling.

Left:
Interior view of the wooden corridor of the Hongjun Bridge showing the stone slab floor and the stone column bases that support a traditional wooden frame.

Left:
Old stone stelae from temples and ancestral halls were re-carved with slogans the Red Army used to raise the politi-cal consciousness of those they moved among the peas-ants and townspeople.

Top:
Many of the shops leading to the bridge have signs declaring they served as billets for Red Army commanders and troops in 1935.

Above:
Also painted red is the structure now housing the Qinglinkou temple, which houses a broad assortment of deities.

Right:
With "Red Army Bridge" em-blazoned not only above it but a commemorative stone plaque below stating the same thing, in addition to other Communist symbols, the abundant traditional ornamentation under the eaves has been allowed to fade and become illegible.

JIEMEI BRIDGES

ANXIAN, SICHUAN

Driving today along some of the mountain highways 180 kilometers northwest of Chengdu to the west of the city of Mianyang in Sichuan province, an occasional billboard portrays the existence of the Jiemei (Sisters) Bridges, but one must search hard for the tiny dirt footpath that eventually opens up to what is undoubtedly a pair of actively used mountain bridges of inimitable beauty. Unlike in the fertile, intensely cultivated lowlands of western Sichuan where human effort in controlling water and enriching soil allows three crops a year—two of rice and a third of vegetables—supporting some of China's densest populations, life in the surrounding mountains has always been arduous. Mountain villagers struggle to wrest a livelihood from the forested slopes along which they live, as well as from the rushing streams that pour down the hillsides. In areas of rugged terrain, life for villagers was rarely bound to the immediate environs of their dwellings, but rather

coursed along steep and windy paths along which men and women sought the bounty of the forests—logs, wild food plants, medicinal roots, bark, and herbs, and wild animals—for their own use as well as for collecting and transporting to sometimes-distant markets. Mountain paths frequently encounter ravines, sometimes filled with rapidly flowing streams, that must be crossed in order to convey raw materials carried on shoulder poles or in baskets on peasants' backs. It is this geographical context within which the Jiemei Bridges took shape.

Throughout western China in the past, as elsewhere in hilly regions of the world, timbers that fell naturally or were intentionally felled and then placed across streams became, in effect, "bridges." With little thought given to design or aesthetics, spans of this nature—mere logs—served as necessary workaday links along the mountain byways. Log bridges of this type, of course, have severe limitations, not only because of rotting due to contact with soil and often infestation by wood-eating insects but also because of the fact that fallen timbers are not necessarily long enough to span a needed gap. The circumstances that may lead eventually to the building of a bridge, let alone decisions made to impart a pleasing aesthetic to the bridge structure, are often lost in the murkiness of history. Yet, as the discovery of hidden bridges of great beauty attests, even those people living in remote areas sometimes quietly experimented with materials to successfully create masterpieces of carpentry that match functionality with beauty.

Overhanging a narrow gap about 10 meters above the bed of the Xiaocha River in Xiaobei township in Anxian county, the Jiemei (Sisters) Bridges are a twinned pair of covered spans that share a common midstream pier, in reality an angled stone outcrop that juts upward between them. Throughout much of the year, the stream languishes gently beneath as the water flows downhill. In spring, however, waters frequently rise abruptly as they disgorge melt water from the uplands. Moreover, when accompanied by continuous heavy spring rains, periodic inundations are known to sweep away fallen trees and other detritus with great destructive force. The striations etched into the rock walls that line the Xiaocha River suggest the magnitude of continuing scouring over the years by swiftly flowing water.

Below left:
Having just walked down from a mountain path to cross the Jiemei Bridges, this local villager regularly enters the woodland in quest of local herbs, medicinal roots, and bark, which he carries in the basket on his back as well as in his hand.

Right:
Glimpsed along the sides of the bridges, the simplicity of construction is apparent: elongated timbers resting on stone abutments; a timber framework notched into the horizontal logs; sawn lumber used as planking; a vertical timber fence; a tiled capped roof set on a mortise-and-tenoned framework; and elevated entryways at each end.

Above:
Sharing an angled stone outcrop that juts up from the streambed below and serves as a pier between them, the two bridges of differing lengths create a scene of sublime beauty.

Left:
With a symmetrical façade comprised of horizontal and vertical timber components capped by a double-tiered roof with uplifted corners, the bridges provide a dramatic passage for those working in the mountains. The commemorative plaque, a recent addition, declares the structure as "The Sisters' Bridges."

Right:
As a pedestrian leaves one bridge corridor, it is necessary to descend a set of stone steps to the outcrop before rising to the second bridge.

Above:
Although the two bridges face each other, it is necessary to use stone steps in order to cross the outcrop between them.

Right:
Walking along a nearby mountain path that follows the line of the river, it is possible to glimpse the pair of bridges through the clumps of bamboo.

Opposite below:
During recent reconstruction of the bridge, old timbers were replaced by newer ones, which have not yet weathered. The auspicious red cloths wrapped around the ridgepoles were attached during the beam raising ceremony.

Above:
While most of the timber members are without carving of any type, on the end of each bridge there are vertical elements with simple carved ornamentation.

Right:
In addition to supporting the roof, each of the columns serves to "lock" horizontal wooden members in place using tenons, pieces of wood shaped at the end for insertion into a mortise to make a joint.

While records indicate that a set of stone bridges existed in this location as early as the twelfth century, it was not until 1873 that the local villagers combined their labor and financial resources to fashion the bridges seen today. The longer bridge, referred to as "elder sister" and the shorter one as "younger sister," are similar in structure and appearance, differing mainly in details. Each end is entered from a mountain path by a series of stone steps leading to a covered bridge constructed using the same carpentry techniques employed in building common homes and temples. Mortise-and-tenoned joinery—without metal nails—is used to lock the twenty-four columns to an uncounted number of beams, roof timbers, and flanking balustrades made up of simple rails and posts, to give shape to a corridor. Approximately 3 meters wide, the flooring is covered with rough-cut planks while the structure overall is capped with baked roof tiles.

In April 2005, some sixty engineers, architects, historians, as well as local boosters came together to proclaim the importance of preserving the Jiemei Bridges, which had been declared a provincial-level architectural landmark. Providing not only a critical cross-water link along a rural byway, the bridges offer a pleasantly cool place to rest and situate oneself within what is undoubtedly a picturesque landscape.

ANLAN SUSPENSION BRIDGE

DUJIANGYAN, GUANXIAN, AND SICHUAN

In Sichuan province, on the western edge of the Chengdu plain, is China's legendary Dujiangyan irrigation system, an ingeniously developed comprehensive network of diversion channels, weirs, canals, and sluice gates. Begun in 250 BCE, this water conservancy system has brought two millennia of prosperity to an area with a population greater than any European country. Control of the torrents of water pouring out of the Tibetan Plateau via the Min River, the longest tributary of the Chang Jiang or Yangzi River, and its own numerous tributaries, is one of the great narratives of technological achievement in Chinese history. Lesser known than the building of the irrigation systems themselves were the efforts made to span both narrow and sometimes quite broad watercourses with suspension bridges.

The Anlan (Tranquil Ripples) Suspension Bridge, also called the Zhupu Bridge, is one of the most famous suspension bridges in China. It not only was a critical component needed for maintenance of the Dujiangyan water conservancy system, providing a vital link in the region's transport system, but also had "buildings" associated with it. Although its actual date of construction is unknown, the bridge existed well before the Song dynasty and may have emerged in the early years when the Dujiangyan system itself took shape in the third century BCE. Having undergone many modifications in length and number of spans over the centuries, the suspension bridge today has a total length of 320 meters and is held aloft by nine piers to overcome the sagging inherent in bridging such a gap. Of the eight suspended spans, the longest is 61 meters. A central granite pier on an island in the river complements a pair of substantial stone abutments at both ends, which serve as anchorages in order to stabilize what otherwise would be a perpetually swaying structure. The pier and the terminal abutments incorporate simple buildings atop them that add not only additional weight but also visual beauty to the line of the suspension bridge itself.

Twenty hefty plaited bamboo cables or ropes, each more than 10 centimeters thick, were originally attached to the anchorage components, ten along the bottom and five on each side. Each of the side cables as well as the bottom cables was threaded through the anchorages and attached to spindles and levers, operating like a winch, that could tighten the cables

Pages 156–7:
When viewed close up, it is clear that traditional materials were not used when the Anlan (Tranquil Ripples) Bridge was rebuilt in 1975. Steel wire cables 25 millimeters thick were employed as balustrades to replace what were once plaited bamboo ropes.

Above:
Today, the suspension bridge is 320 meters in length, held aloft by nine prestressed masonry piers designed to overcome the sagging inherent in crossing the broad Minjiang River with its rushing torrents.

Left:
On display near the bridge are replicas of many of the devices used to control waters in the Dujiangyan irrigation system, including these elongated bamboo "cages" filled with rocks, as well as weighted-down tripods that were used seasonally to direct the flow of the water.

as needed. Helping to lift the cables and keep the transverse wooden plank decking relatively horizontal were six intermediate timber trestle piers formed from log-cribs set upon stone bases sunk into the riverbed. A system of bamboo and wooden frames gripped the side cables and kept those crossing from falling over the side. For much of its history, no metal was employed in any part of the bridge, although elsewhere in southwest China wrought iron chains began to be used with shorter suspension bridges as early as the sixth century. For the Anlan Bridge, a nearby grove of bamboo was essentially all that was needed to provide replacement materials as the structure aged. For several months each year, the bridge would be closed to traffic for maintenance because of the need to replace disintegrating bamboo and wood as well as accommodate changes in the river channel. Every three years, the bamboo cables themselves were replaced with new ones.

Fan Chengda, a late twelfth-century traveler, recorded in his diary not only his admiration for the scale of the Anlan Suspension Bridge but also his anxiety and fear of falling into the seething water beneath: "When there is a strong wind, it sways up and down. It is like the nets strung out by fishermen for drying, or the loops of coloured silk suspended by the dyers. I had to give up my litter, and walked across swiftly in a manner which might have seemed

graceful, but really I was trembling so much that I could hardly stand upright. All my company turned pale ...." (quoted in Needham, 4(3): 192–3).

At the end of the Ming dynasty, in order to frustrate advances in a peasant uprising, the bridge was severely damaged and river crossings were only possible via ferries. In 1802, the suspension bridge was rebuilt, it is said, through the efforts of a husband and wife team who read the records of travelers like Fan Chengda for guidance in its reconstruction. Unfortunately, because of insufficient capital, inadequate materials, and negligent construction, cables on the bridge broke, sending passersby to their death. After the wife took leadership in its restoration, the Anlan Bridge became known also as the Fuqi (Husband and Wife) Bridge because of the devoted couple who had taken the lead in building it.

Once mule packs loaded with coal, wheelbarrows laden with goods, and laborers carrying commodities on shoulder poles kept the bridge crowded and swaying, but now no longer. The Anlan Suspension Bridge was rebuilt in 1975 using durable 25 millimeter thick steel wire cables and prestressed concrete piers that preserve the traditional appearance, especially when seen from a distance, while maintaining—for pedestrian tourists who visit Dujiangyan—a semblance of the unnerving sway that had been the suspension bridge's hallmark for nearly 2,000 years.

Above:
On top of each of the piers through which the cables pass is a small roofed structure, which serves more an ornamental than a functional purpose.

BRIDGES IN THE LOWER YANGZI WATERTOWNS

JIANGSU, SHANGHAI, AND ZHEJIANG

Countless canals and canalside villages and towns crisscross the Jiangnan or "South of the Yangzi River" region in central China. During the Sui dynasty in the early years of the seventh century, this fertile rice bowl area was connected via what became known as the Grand Canal in order to facilitate the efficient transport of grain to the imperial capital region in northern China. Called "the countryside of fish and rice" (*yu mi zhi xiang*) by the Chinese because of the richness of its agricultural production, the water-laced Jiangnan region has long been known for its robust commercialized market-oriented economy linking countless villages, towns, and cities. As both wealth and population increased, prosperity nurtured a refined literati culture noted not only for its artistic tastes but also for the impact of these inclinations on the material landscape in terms of distinctive dwellings, temples, ancestral halls, academies, gardens, and myriad, sometimes sublime, bridges.

To geographers and historians, the Jiangnan region, which includes placid Lake Tai and extends from Nanjing eastward to Shanghai, is as remarkable for its maze-like hydrography as it is for its rather level topography. Between settlements, the Jiangnan landscape is relatively low and flat, usually only 3–5 meters above sea level. Most of the land is made up of paddy fields separated from each other by slightly elevated embankments because of the constant threat of inundation during wet periods of the year.

Indeed, it is the interplay between the fragmented low-lying patches of land and the ever-present nearby water areas—veritable arteries of people's livelihood—that provided the rhythm for traditional life. No structures epitomize this interdependence more than bridges, which are conspicuous landmarks everywhere in the region. Bridges help stitch the fragmented landscape into a functioning mosaic of irrigated fields lined with perennial bushes and trees, such as mulberry, tea, masson pine, and fruits.

Until recently, it was easiest to reach watertowns and small villages throughout the Jiangnan area by small boat rather than car or bus, being sculled or rowed along canals of different widths, first along the broader arteries and then the slender veins. Superimposed upon this dense pattern of water passageways was a system of footpaths—sometimes more or less paved with flagstones but more often merely a compacted track of earth—that connected small settlements and provided access for peasants to their fields and ponds. This combination of canals and footpaths led inevitably to the building of countless bridges so that both foot traffic and boat traffic could be optimized, neither being disadvantaged by the activities of the other.

While low horizontal stone or wooden beam bridges certainly could ease passage across a narrow canal and were economical to "build," such bridging structures clearly blocked boat traffic. Out of necessity, alternatives emerged. In some cases, stone slabs were piled in stepped layers on both sides of a canal and then topped with a beam that effectively elevated the span. When the innovative use of an arch was first employed in this region is not known, but it is certain that humpbacked bridges with steep stepped approaches eased canal passage while not seriously impacting pedestrians even though they were impassable for wheeled carts. The ubiquity of semicircular arched stone bridges of many dimensions points to ongoing experimentation with both materials and designs in order to meet particular local needs. While there are similarities among different bridges, each clearly is original. Even in recent times, innovations continue to be made that test the properties of stone and cement as well as mitigate shortcomings in original structures. One minor, but hardly inconsequential improvement found on old bridges with steep steps has been the embedding of narrow strips of cement along the treads of the steps so that cyclists can push their light-framed wheeled vehicles over the bridge. Western travelers in China in early times were as captivated by the sight of peasants with their overloaded shoulder poles as they were with the many types of shallow-draft vessels seen on the canals. Their photographs taken along both pathways and

Left and right:
Originally built during the Yuan dynasty but altered many times during the Ming and Qing dynasties, the granite Ruyi (Whatever You Want) Bridge is 20.8 meters long and 3.4 meters wide.

Above right:
The Huimin (Benefit the People) Bridge near by retains some of the characteristics of the Ruyi Bridge but on a smaller scale.

canals, often near a bridge, are testaments to the seeming omnipresence of all the critical elements of the traditional transportation system.

Chinese straightforwardly refer to the Jiangnan watertown areas, where virtually all of the original woodlands and marshes have been extinguished, as *shuixiang* or "water country." Once there were hundreds of villages and towns within the Jiangnan canal network, and thus thousands of sometimes lofty bridges stood as visually prominent markers within the landscape. In the 1930s, Fugl-Meyer estimated that there were upwards of eight bridges per square kilometer along the intricate network of canals in the single province of Jiangsu, which constitutes a large part of the Jiangnan region. The prefectural government in the city of Suzhou in the late Qing dynasty not only had jurisdiction over 309 bridges within the city's walls, but also maintained some 700 others in the environs outside (1937: 32).

In a rush to modernize and industrialize over the past quarter century, far too many traditional settlements were hastily sacrificed when their past forms and identity were erased with the filling in of canals and ponds, the construction of roads, and the dismantling of old neighborhoods, in the process destroying the houses, shops, temples, and teahouses

Above and left:
This grand pavilion, with a double-tiered roof with upturned eaves, is new construction atop the gate near the Feng (Maple) Bridge.

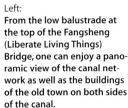

Left:
From the low balustrade at the top of the Fangsheng (Liberate Living Things) Bridge, one can enjoy a panoramic view of the canal network as well as the buildings of the old town on both sides of the canal.

Below left:
Constructed between 1265 and 1274 during the Song dynasty, and the oldest bridge in Shanghai, the Puji (Universal Salvation) Bridge is one of very few bridges built using purple-colored stone, called *zishi* in Chinese.

Below right:
The 34-meter-long Yingxiang (Welcoming Blessings) Bridge, built between 1335 and 1340 during the Yuan dynasty of cut-stone planks and fired bricks, rises like an arched structure over the water.

that gave them character. Countless centuries-old bridges, touted as old-fashioned and useless, were destroyed, swept away by the scythe of progress. Few of the proliferating new houses, factories, and workshops that replaced the old forms echo anything at all that might be called "Chinese."

Some attention to the conservation of a few of the Jiangnan watertowns began in the 1980s even as the annihilation of most of what had served as traditional cultural landscape features proceeded apace. It is doubtful that anyone foresaw that two decades later, at the beginning of the twenty-first century, there could possibly be reasonably successful heritage preservation in the watertown region. As signature pieces in the composition of all watertowns, bridges and the canals they cross have received special attention by those setting out to preserve the character of the watertowns, leading not only to the restoration of many old bridges but also the creation of many new ones in old styles. While it is sometimes difficult to differentiate the truly old bridges from the newer structures, it is still possible, even as the twenty-first century begins, to experience authentic expressions of China's past in the dozen or so watertowns. Waterside pavilions, quaint teahouses, temples, memorial arches, high stone bridges—most at human scale—

contribute to a generally slower pace of life, which is welcomed by visitors as well as residents who desire a taste of life in China's past.

Among the most noteworthy extant watertowns with restored sections are Luzhi, Tongli, and Zhouzhuang in Jiangsu province, and Nanxun, Wuzhen, and Xitang in Zhejiang province, which have been put forward as a group for designation as a UNESCO World Heritage Site. Sadly, many others have been developed beyond recognition as watertowns. Others are in various states of preservation, especially Jinze, Qingpu, and Zhujiajiao within metropolitan Shanghai; Anchang, Dongpu, and Keqiao near Shaoxing in eastern Zhejiang; and Guangfu, Jinxi, Mudu, and Shaxi near Suzhou in southern Jiangsu. Most of these Jiangnan watertowns are within a couple hours of Shanghai, China's mega city, and thus have already felt the impact of swelling visitation. Chinese tourists, of course, dominate tourism in China, enticed to remote locations by websites, news reports, word of mouth, and increasing affluence. With the acceleration of domestic tourism in China, threats of overuse present daunting challenges, a subject that unfortunately cannot be addressed here. Rather, the sections below, as elsewhere in the book, focus on bridges, with only suggestions to the reader of broader issues.

Zhujiajiao, Shanghai

Zhujiajiao (Zhu Family Corner), once a watertown adrift in the "water country" on the bank of Lake Dianshan, has now been absorbed into the built-up suburbs of the sprawling metropolis of Shanghai. It is thus easily accessible to some 20 million people via a quick one-hour ride on a high-speed expressway just 50 kilometers from the city center. Zhujiajiao developed as a strategic watertown in the Ming dynasty and reached its prime as a bustling market in the 1930s. Its economic prosperity arose from the settlement's centrality within the extensive network of canals that brought unhulled rice from the surrounding farms to some seventy rice shops in the town where it was processed for dispersal to other parts of China.

The old section of Zhujiajiao covers a mere 2.7 square kilometers, a tiny fraction of the much larger modern urban settlement surrounding it. Although once there were thirty-six bridges sprinkled throughout the town's canals, today only twenty remain, among them stone beam, stone arch, brick, and wood structures.

The most celebrated bridge in Zhujiajiao is the magnificent Fangsheng (Liberate Living Things) Bridge over the Caogang River that was built in 1571, reputedly under the leadership of a monk, Xing Chao, of the Cimen Temple, who raised the necessary funds and organized the construction. Xing Chao also organized a *fangsheng she*, a small organization whose purpose it was to "liberate living things" following the Buddhist admonition, "Among all negative karma, that of killing is the heaviest. Among all positive karma, that for releasing life is the highest." It was at the foot of the new Fangsheng Bridge that a fenced-in pool was constructed for devotees to set fish free in order to gain merit; hence the bridge acquired not only its name but gained prominence in the community for its noble purpose.

On the first day of every month during the lunar calendar, devout men and women came to the bridge to release fish as well as other animals. On important festivals throughout the year, the bridge was used as a "stage" for celebrations. At no time was anyone permitted to fish using nets or poles or even anchor their fishing boats in the

Above:
Few bridges in the Jiangnan watertown region are as famous as Zhujiajiao's splendid Fangsheng (Liberate Living Things) Bridge, which was constructed in 1571 over the Caogang River. Spanning 72 meters, it is the longest five-arch bridge still standing in China.

Right:
The approach to the Fangsheng Bridge is via a set of sloping steps with minimal risers that ease the passage of those carrying heavy loads.

Below:
The Huimin (Benefit the People) Bridge, which had existed in the past and was reconstructed in 1996, is the only covered timber frame corridor span in Zhujiajiao.

Bottom:
As the centerpiece of the level portion at the summit of the Fangsheng Bridge is a low-relief carved *samsara*, a stylized shape representing the Buddhist belief in an eternal cycle of birth, suffering, death, and rebirth. Stones of this type are called *longmen* or Dragon Gate stones.

immediate environs of the bridge. Today, old ladies wearing traditional rural outfits line up to sell visitors transparent plastic bags filled with water and goldfish, which they can set free and gain merit. Inscriptions on the weather-scarred steles alongside the river remind townsfolk that it is an act of compassion to do good deeds, including liberating animals, in order to accumulate merit for the afterlife.

Some 72 meters long and 5 meters wide, the Fangsheng Bridge is the largest five-arch bridge still standing in China. With an imposing height of 7.4 meters, pedestrians must climb several scores of stone steps before reaching the summit, from where they can enjoy the breeze and a pleasant view. Atop the bridge are stone tablets called Dragon Gate stones since they are engraved with eight coiling dragons encircling a shining pearl. Four lifelike stone lions sit upon pillars along the top balusters.

Right:
Throughout Zhujiajiao, as in other watertowns, beautiful bridges are best appreciated while being sculled on a small boat plying the canals framed by old dwellings and shops.

Far right:
This narrow elevated stone beam bridge is lined with hewn timbers.

Tongli, Jiangsu

Surrounded by lakes on all sides and adjacent to Lake Tai, Tongli's spatial layout is one that honors water, yet one does not need a map to enjoy it. All the visitor needs to do is wander in order to serendipitously experience what is in many ways an authentic contemporary outpost that echoes simpler times. Throughout much of the town, the slabstone lanes parallel the canals, with houses and shops set back from the water. At the heart of the old town, the canals effectively divide the town into seven small islands linked by nearly fifty stone bridges in a variety of styles. Beyond this core area, there are numerous other canals and islands with linking bridges with poetic names.

The oldest bridge in Tongli is Siben (Reflecting Origin) Bridge, built during the Song dynasty. The smallest span, only 1.5 meters long and less than a meter wide, is called Dubu (Single Step) Bridge. It is the composition of three nearby bridges that has become the signature of Tongli: the small and exquisite Taiping (Peace and Tranquility) Bridge built early in the nineteenth century; Jili (Luck) Bridge, an arched bridge inscribed with couplets describing the beautiful painting-like views at either end; and Changqing (Continuous Celebration) Bridge, also named Guangli Bridge, first constructed in 1470 and rebuilt in 1704. During important occasions, such as weddings and birthdays, townspeople make a transit of all three bridges, which together form a ring, as an invocation wishing peace, good fortune, and general happiness.

Above:
With one of Tongli's many fine stone bridges behind her, a local fisherwoman holds a cormorant, which she has trained to dive for fish.

Below:
The Jili (Luck) Bridge and the nearby Taiping Bridge and Changqing Bridge, together form the nodes of a triangular circuit that local folk pass over to celebrate grand occasions.

Right:
With its level approaches and expansive breadth, this triple-arch bridge is clearly a modern structure built to accommodate the passage of vehicles, which, on the day this photograph was taken, were banned from the area to ease movement by visitors.

Below right:
The San'an Bridge in Tongli is a stone beam bridge shaped in such a way that the outer portions are thicker than the central portion.

Left:
The Wujin (Black/Crow Gold) Bridge, originally built in 1811 and until fairly recently situated amidst rice fields on the outskirts of the built-up area, was restored at its present location within Tongli as an additional elegant reminder of sophisticated stone arch bridge building.

Below left:
This *longmen* stone on the central span of a bridge is inscribed with a pair of fish, two carp, pronounced as *shuang yu*, with the homophonous meaning "doubled prosperity."

Bottom left:
Here, the *longmen* stone is a simplified *samsara*, a Buddhist emblem representing the continuing cycle of birth and rebirth.

Below:
This rather small arch bridge crosses a narrow canal, which like others in Tongli, is confined by stone walls and lined with narrow slabstone lanes.

Above:
Viewed from along the canal, the restored Wujin (Black/Crow Gold) Bridge is situated at a purposely designed scenic spot with an adjacent pavilion and old trees.

Right:
With a pavilion atop its central stone beam span, this bridge in Tongli is also raised by a pair of small arches. Strollers can sit on the stone balustrades to enjoy the breezes and the shade.

Wuzhen, Zhejiang

Situated along the Grand Canal in northeastern Zhejiang, Wuzhen is threaded through by narrow canals that straddle the watery border between Zhejiang and Jiangsu provinces. Only open to visitors since 2001, Wuzhen is unlike some of the better-known watertowns since little of it has undergone restoration except for those surrounding the public entry area where a recently restored soaring *pailou* or ceremonial archway leads to a high stage for Chinese opera performances. Adjacent portions designated as part of the historic area are being developed with an emphasis on improving infrastructure, including placing water pipes and electric wires underground, repairing old walkways, removing newer structures, and assisting long-time residents to move out of the area to new housing. A prominently restored area is one called "workshop area," with individual shops producing and selling rice wine, dried red tobacco, dyed cotton, cotton shoes, as well as rattan, bamboo, and wood products. For the most part, the old buildings remain in a noteworthy state of preservation. Life in Wuzhen is much as it was in the past, with remarkably few buildings specifically serving tourists. Walking along any of the narrow lanes, one easily glimpses the rhythms of daily life—carting fresh

water, cooking meals, tending to young children, and playing mahjong. Local workshops continue to make wine, homespun cotton, as well as other items made of wood, silk, and metal.

The historic area of Wuzhen is currently 1.3 square kilometers in size, with many two-storey houses having their fronts along a lane and their backs against a canal; many structures function both as shops or workshops as well as residences. The patina of unpainted aged wood complements well the other natural surfaces of cut gray granite foundations, dark roof tiles, and mottled whitewashed stepped gable walls. Many of the shop-dwelling structures are raised on piers over the adjacent canal and have steps leading down to a stone landing providing access to passing boats selling goods, but also where a boat can be tied or laundry washed.

There are about 120 old bridges of one type or other throughout Wuzhen. The so-called Bridge-Within-a-Bridge, actually a pair of bridges, deserves special mention. One of the bridges, the Tongji (Crossing) Bridge, was constructed in 1514 with a single arch spanning nearly 12 meters, a length of 28 meters, and a width of 3.5 meters, while the other bridge, built in 1518 and called Renji (Benevolence in Abundance) Bridge, has a length of nearly 23 meters,

Below:
The Wanxing (All Things Flourishing) Bridge, with an overall length of 19.7 meters, has central stone beams that exceed 10 meters.

Right:
Fitted tightly amidst the waterside houses at a junction of two canals, the Yixiu (Pouring Out Elegance) Bridge is a modest cut-stone bridge about which there is little information.

a width of 2.8 meters, and a span of 8.5 meters. A distinctive feature of these two bridges is that either can be seen through the arch of the other, hence the name Bridge-Within-a-Bridge. Both bridges rise quite high so that pedestrians must climb more than twenty steps to cross them.

Wuzhen is a reasonably tranquil town although it has an impressive vitality. While many residents have moved out of the old town to new high-rise apartments, those who have stayed, mainly the elderly but also numerous younger entrepreneurs, take pride in the many traditional goods and services that provide a distinctiveness to the watertown: *sanbai* ("three white") wine, which is made from white glutinous rice, "white flour" (distiller's yeast), and "white water," that is, clean water; blue-dyed indigo cotton; shadow puppet shows in which the "actors" are crafted from the hides of oxen and sheep. While only a fraction of the seventy teahouses that were once in Wuzhen remain, those that do continue to offer opportunities to slow the pace of one's life while enjoying the fussily brewed teas.

Above:
The original stone Yingjia (Ying Family) Bridge, located at the center of the traditional commercial core of Wuzhen, and dating to the eighteenth century, was replaced in the 1920s by a concrete bridge that was able to carry vehicular traffic. The "ancient" bridge seen today is a reconstruction that was added as the town was developed for tourism.

Shaoxing, Zhejiang

Located just to the south of Hangzhou Bay within a "water country" similar to that north of the bay, Shaoxing has a longer and more glorious history than most Jiangnan watertowns. Some 2,000 years ago, Shaoxing, then known as Guiji, was the capital of the Yue kingdom during the Spring and Autumn period, and it is said that Yu the Great, a legendary emperor, learned to control floods in the environs of Shaoxing some 5,000 years before that. Yu the Great's mausoleum near by remains a special place of veneration.

Shaoxing today is a modern city of nearly 350,000 people surrounded by economic development zones. Even if most of the traces of its earlier existence as a watertown are long gone, the city still retains sites of historic significance, including scores of homes of illustrious residents, such as Xu Wei, a Ming-dynasty calligrapher, painter, poet, and dramatist, and Lu Xun, a progressive twentieth-century author. None of the watertowns near Shaoxing, such as Anchang, Dongpu, and Keqiao, has received the kind of investment in preservation seen in other Jiangnan watertowns farther north, and thus all have had their historical cores impinged upon by modern industrial development. Nonetheless, each has a number of slow-moving canals with busy boat traffic and vestiges of traditional commerce mixed with what is modern.

No bridge in Shaoxing is more important than the Bazi Bridge, built during the later Song dynasty in 1256, and reputedly the oldest extant urban bridge in China. Found at the junction of three canals and three lanes, the structure is actually comprised of two juxtaposed bridges that are reminiscent of the Chinese character representing the number eight. Four-meter-long stone columns form the abutments and rest on a double layer of quarried stone 1.8 meters thick, which in turn is set atop a foundation of stone boulders. The principal span clears 4.5 meters, is slightly cambered, and has a width of 3.2 meters. Together with the balustrades and approach steps, the bridge is assembled from countless quarried slabs forming a structure of incalculable weight and substantial versatility that fits compactly into a tight residential environment.

Above:
Said to be the oldest extant urban bridge in China, the Bazi (Character Eight) Bridge in Shaoxing was built in 1256 during the later Song dynasty. Located where three canals and three lanes converge, the bridge is made up of two conjoined stone beam spans, which function much like overpasses across multiple streets do today, and together suggest the Chinese character for the number eight.

Opposite far left:
Circular forms like these are used to buttress the balusters of many Jiangnan bridges.

Opposite left:
One of the many approaches to the Bazi Bridge, this one is narrow yet allows both pedestrians and carts to use it.

Left:
As with other bridges in the Jiangnan region, sloped surfaces have been added to the treads of the Bazi Bridge to facilitate the passage of two-wheeled carts and bicycles.

Bridges in the Lower Yangzi Watertowns **177**

Above:
The Taiping (Heavenly Peace) Bridge, located some 16 kilometers west of Shaoxing along an extension of the Grand Canal, combines a soaring arch that rises 7 meters with a series of beam spans that together cross 24.2 meters of water.

Left:
The series of nine stone beam bridges progressively decrease in height as they stretch out from the arched portion of the Taiping Bridge towards the north bank of the canal.

Right:
The detail of the balustrades along the steps includes interconnected *wan* characters, which mean "longevity."

The Taiping (Heavenly Peace) Bridge, which spans an extension of the Grand Canal running from Hangzhou to Ningbo, is located some 16 kilometers west of Shaoxing. Considered one of the region's most beautiful bridges, it is a combination bridge with a soaring arch as well as a series of nine stone beam spans that together cross 24.2 meters of water. The bridge seen today was constructed in 1858, a successor structure of ones built in 1622 and 1741. Approached from the south by a paired set of steps that form a T-shape from the waterside towpath, the semicircular arch of the bridge rises 7 meters above the canal below. The bridge is well known for its beautifully ornamented and elegantly carved stone panels and posts. On the northern side of the bridge, there once was a temple, now long gone, and recently replaced with a museum of bridges.

In each of these watertowns, daily life continues even as the modern world intrudes, although there are differences between the old and new areas of the towns. Indeed, each has a nearby "new town" with multistoried apartment blocks, schools, factories, and shopping centers, considered more comfortable and convenient than the tightly packed quarters of the old town. On the main streets in the newer sections, cars and buses increase in number even as in the back alleys pedestrians, some carrying shoulder poles, and bicycles dominate. Along the granite-paved lanes lined with two-storey wooden shophouses, men, women, and children continue to shop for fresh produce, chat with neighbors, cart water, cook meals, clean out their buckets, and tend their flower pots. Artisans work in many old workshops producing objects made of copper, wood, cotton, silk, and paper. Sometimes during the busy midday, visitors overrun the old watertowns to the degree that neither their charm nor their inherited markers from the past—buildings, canals, and, especially, bridges—can be appreciated.

In recent years, the physical and economic transformation of the broader "water country" beyond Shanghai has accelerated, leaving the remaining historic watertowns adrift in a sea of hurried change. "One City, Nine Towns" has become the mantra for the urban/suburban expansion of Shanghai, with at least nine satellite "new towns" being built. All of this is purportedly part of a comprehensive plan based upon sustainable development principles, including attention to transit-oriented development and historic preservation. Somewhat bizarrely, new international forms of canal towns are emerging to replace traditional ones. Each town is to be a "concept town" in which the layout and architecture are *not* to be derived from Chinese antecedents, but instead to reflect foreign settlement forms, or some ingredients of those forms, producing a veritable European Union of new towns: a British, Dutch, German, Swedish, Spanish, Italian, Canadian, Australian/New Zealand, as well as two American-style towns. Zhujiajiao is planned to be a Chinese town. While these audacious ideas have been mocked by many, substantial aspects of the plan have already been successfully implemented. Somewhat noticeably, canals and bridges—each in the national style of the concept country—figure prominently, thus creating new forms for an old architectural vocabulary.

SUZHOU AND HANGZHOU GARDEN BRIDGES

JIANGSU AND ZHEJIANG

Nowhere more than in a Chinese garden or park can a bridge be understood in its often simultaneous manifestations as structural object, defined place, transitional passage, and versatile ornament. Like an individual rockery or ponded water, a bridge in a garden is rarely merely decorative. As depicted in images throughout this book, their form fluctuates from the simple to the complex; their material varies in terms of strength; their scale ranges from the miniature to the dominating; their route may be purposefully straight, curved, or zigzagged. As a component in a synthesis of elements in a designed landscape composition, bridges are able to echo and enhance their surroundings. Sometimes mimicking natural features, garden and park bridges allude to the aesthetic values found in nature. Often a bridge helps divide scenery while being itself a spectacular scene. The historical and geographical complexity of China frustrates any attempt to speak of a quintessential garden or park bridge. As the examples below show, bridges in gardens and parks are never an afterthought.

No area of China has more private gardens—often called classical, literati, or scholars' gardens—than the Jiangnan region, the water-laced lower reaches of the Chang Jiang (Yangzi River), and no city in the region has more celebrated gardens than Suzhou. Nearby cities such as Yangzhou, Changzhou, Huzhou, Hangzhou, Wuxi, and Shanghai also have good examples, but they are generally less known and less visited than those in Suzhou. Indeed, hundreds of small and large private gardens survive throughout the low-lying delta region, including those in canalside villages and towns such as Wuzhen, Nanxun, and Xitang in Zhejiang province and Guangfu, Jinxi, Luzhi, Mudu, Tongli, and Zhouzhuang in Jiangsu province. Distinctive private gardens, rich in regional character, are found also in significant numbers in the well-watered Red Basin of western Sichuan province as well as in the Pearl River Delta of Guangdong province. Over the past decade, the promise of booming tourism has led to the restoration of once seemingly lost gardens that had either been allowed to decay over the years because of lack of maintenance or had been destroyed because of warfare or anti-bourgeois attitudes during the Great Proletarian Cultural Revolution.

Jiangnan Gardens

Wherever the Jiangnan garden, each is an ingenious composition with its own idiosyncratic composition and endless variations of buildings, water features, rocks, plants, and, of course, bridges. Often found down narrow dead-end alleys and hidden behind high walls, small spaces were enlarged by "borrowing the sky" that rose above a body of water or beyond a wall. Bridges, like paths and rockeries, not only constituted parts of scenes but were a means to move forward or above, vehicles for positioning a person in order to glimpse or gather a view. Chen Congzhou, the noted Chinese landscape connoisseur and chronicler of Jiangnan architecture, coined the terms "static viewing" and "dynamic viewing" to describe the experience of movement and place within Chinese gardens. In smaller gardens with shorter bridges, visitors find themselves at spots from which to focus on specific views from relatively fixed angles. Such places invite one to stand or sit, to tarry or move, but always to contemplate. By purposefully positioning meandering paths and zigzag bridges, strollers are enticed to visually assemble a moving panorama from ever-changing angles at each step of the way. Walking on uneven bridges of rock, stone, bamboo, or timber, the visitor is able to "nourish the heart" by being led to unexpected sites. Bridges are sometimes mere planks

of rough-cut stone, flanking logs, or strategically placed stepping stones. Walls confine some bridges in order to define a spatial composition. Straight lines contrast with curved edges as bridges lead to promontories or islets, just as dark spaces contrast with bright spaces. The ever-changing mirroring effect of water helps heighten the feeling of spaciousness even in small gardens, generating fragments comparable to the voids, or unpainted spaces, of Chinese monochromatic paintings. As both artifact and artifice, garden bridges, like other elements of the Chinese garden, are deliberately imbued with meaning as nature is re-created in microcosm.

The expansive Zhuozheng Yuan (Garden of the Humble Administrator) and the compact Liu Yuan (Lingering Garden) illustrate contrasting garden types, in general, and the use of bridges, in particular. The site of the Zhuozheng Yuan garden was used as a residence as early as the Tang dynasty (618–907), but garden construction apparently did not begin until 1513 under the supervision of a disgraced Ming-dynasty court historiographer. Most of what one sees today took shape at the end of the nineteenth century. Occupying more than 4 hectares, fully three-fifths of the garden is water, with many types of bridges. There are several simple

Pages 180–1:
The Yudai (Jade Belt) Bridge, with its double-tiered pavilion atop massive stone piers, provides not only a passageway but also a retreat to catch the breezes and enjoy the scenes along West Lake on an offshoot route from the Su Causeway in Hangzhou.

Opposite above and below:
As found in the Zhuozheng Yuan or Garden of the Humble Administrator in Suzhou, these two bridges—single arch and zigzag—are representative of common bridges found throughout gardens in the Jiangnan region. Each is relatively simple in terms of construction technique and quite adaptable to a variety of locations.

Above:
Perhaps the most celebrated bridge in the Garden of the Humble Administrator is the Little Flying Rainbow Bridge, called Xiaofeihong, a rare covered wooden structure set upon a stone beam base that separates two areas of the garden.

stone beam bridges, some with multiple spans, lined with low balustrades that are lifted by hidden stone piers, allowing a passerby to enjoy blooming lotus leafs and flowers rising from the water. Here and there are found single-arch bridges, rather miniature examples of bridges spanning canals outside. Some bridges zigzag, at once seeming to enlarge what is small and extending the experience of a compact space by lengthening the distance between two points. Each segment of a zigzag bridge is as much a pathway—a means of transit—as a vantage point for lingering observation. The stroller is coaxed to move forward by the bends in the bridge, in the process heightening the pleasure of moving from the shore to the several islets in the pond. The highly regarded Xiaofeihong (Little Flying Rainbow) gallery, while simply a span of adjacent stone beams along a wall, is in many ways a bridge, a spanning structure constructed of wood and tile that fully integrates it with the nearby pavilions as it rises above the water. Nearby halls, some open on all sides, as well as pavilions, verandas, corridors, and paths mimic experiences one can gain crossing bridges.

On the other hand, the tiny Liu Yuan or Lingering Garden, which occupies only 2 hectares, was built in the late sixteenth century during the Ming dynasty and then expanded during the Qing dynasty. Situated off a busy street, the residence and garden together afford a sanctuary, a retreat from the world, by the interplay of carefully composed spaces. At the center of the composition is a central pool with modest halls and pavilions clustering around it, especially on the eastern side. Only several locations afford space for small bridges to cross inlets of the water—among these are a plain stone beam bridge barely a meter long and an unpretentious stone arch bridge that leads to a secluded corner. Both bridges have a scale and charm that invite one to linger.

Above:
With the appearance of a covered bridge, this series of spans linking small islets in Liu Yuan or Lingering Garden is actually "roofed" with a trellis-like arbor that is covered with climbing vines.

Right:
Varying in length according to need, simple stone beam bridges set upon short-piled stone planks like this one in the Garden of the Humble Administrator, are common in Jiangnan gardens.

Hangzhou's Parks

Hangzhou, the imperial capital during the Southern Song period (1127–9), is situated at the southern terminus of the Grand Canal amidst "countryside of fish and rice." Embraced by hills, its seductive centerpiece is West Lake, a shallow, irregular, man-made reservoir whose creation and modifications owe much to the efforts of China's great poets like Bai Juyi in the ninth century and Su Dongpo in the eleventh century. Serving also as officials, these poet-administrators built sea walls, dykes, causeways, and bridges in addition to restoring pagodas and temples in order to fashion a landscape that Chinese legend attributes to a pearl dropped to earth from the Milky Way by a dragon and phoenix. Indeed, it was the human-modified beauty of the scenery in Hangzhou that Chinese emperors of the Qing period sought to replicate in their imperial precincts in northern China.

Left:
After a severe frost has turned the lotus leaves brown, an artist finds an enchanting scene of water and plants a month or so before winter sets in, with the Duan (Broken) Bridge) in the background, to create "Lingering Snow on the Broken Bridge," considered one of the poetically lyrical *Ten Scenes of West Lake*.

Below:
This 1633 woodblock print of Hangzhou's West Lake, with the Bai Causeway on the right and the Su Causeway in the middle, prominently features the variety of linking bridges.

Right:
Taken at the end of the nineteenth century, this photograph of the Duan (Broken) Bridge reveals not only the dilapidated state of the Bai Causeway but also the fact that the bridge itself was once much smaller than what is heralded today as an "ancient" structure, as seen on page 186. Moreover, during the Song dynasty, a wooden pavilion rested atop the arch to provide a covered space from which to enjoy the beauty of the West Lake and its surroundings.

Bridges abound in Hangzhou—within temple complexes, in subterranean caves, and in the rugged surrounding hills—but it is those around West Lake, especially along causeways memorializing the city's famous poets, which are most celebrated. A 1633 woodblock print of West Lake clearly shows somewhat uniform arch bridges along both causeways, but over time many of these were altered into distinctive types similar to those seen today.

Along the Bai Causeway are two relatively massive, yet gently rising single-arch bridges—the Duan (Broken) Bridge, sometimes evocatively called Lingering Snow on the Broken Bridge, and the Brocade Belt Bridge—which separate West Lake proper from the North Inner Lake. Lingering Snow on the Broken Bridge, a name that dates to the Tang dynasty, is woven into one of China's most famous stories, the legend of the lady White Snake, which tells the tale of love between a human and an immortal. Today, couples enjoy strolling along the low-lying bridge over the serene lake in any season, whether the bridge has a dusting of snow on it or is surrounded by flowering or fading lotus. The bridge seen today has undergone many changes. During the Song dynasty, a wooden pavilion was built atop it, but that collapsed at some point in history even though the memory of its form was never lost. By the end of the nineteenth century, much of the

Left:
This single-arch stone bridge, with its stone plank approaches, is located on the Su Causeway.

Below:
At the end of the Bai Causeway, connecting Solitary Island with the nearby embankment, the Xiling Bridge is a low single-arch structure, which reminds visitors of the better-known and longer Broken Bridge at the other end of the causeway.

causeway and the bridge had deteriorated significantly, losing much of its historical resonance and utility. The substantial bridge seen today was built in 1941 to meet the needs of modern convenience.

Along the 3-kilometer Su Causeway, which begins in the north opposite the temple dedicated to Yue Fei, six bridges—in contrasting styles—serve not only as set picturesque pieces but also punctuate what might otherwise be a lackluster walk along the fringe of the massive lake. Lined with flowering plants like magnolia, cherry, and hibiscus that will blossom all year around, the causeway is one of the most attractive and poetic sites in the city as one crosses the Reflecting Ripples Bridge, Locking Ripples Bridge, Hill View Bridge, Suppressing-the-Dyke Bridge, East Lake-Mouth Bridge, and Crossing-the-Rainbow Bridge. These six bridges served as patterns for those the Qianlong emperor later built along the West Causeway of his own Summer Palace in Beijing. In the southern portion of West Lake, Xiaoyingzhou appears to be an islet, but actually it is a series of circular embankments that create the appearance of "an island within a lake and a lake within an island." Winding across the enclosed pools of water on Xiaoyingzhou is the well-known Bridge of Nine Bends that leads to one of Hangzhou's ten famous prospects, Three Pools Mirroring the Moon.

In recent years, there has been an extensive expansion of parks adjacent to West Lake. On the east side, the removal of nineteenth and twentieth-century buildings has created a green zone that eventually merges with the commercial heart of the contemporary city. On the west and southern rims of the lake, once-derelict imperial parks have been renewed and new parks have been inserted to the degree that much of Hangzhou remains to be discovered even by those who thought they knew it well. Throughout these parks, old bridges have been reclaimed. In some cases, historic bridges from other locations have been moved into the parks as a way of preserving them. New bridges in old styles also have proliferated.

Wherever gardens and parks are found in China, they are essentially artifactual links to a literati tradition in which scholars used them as places of culture: for contemplation and study, for painting, and calligraphy, as well as for the cultivation of auspicious plants, birds, and fish. While some gardens and parks are sprawling, most resort to elements in miniature in order to aesthetically array necessarily complementary elements into relatively small spaces. Whatever the scale, a characteristic of any Chinese garden or park is the multidimensional spatial interplay of simple, elegant, and poetic components, including bridges, as objects not simply to be viewed but from which to view other places.

WUTING BRIDGE

YANGZHOU, JIANGSU

Unlike most of the understated literati garden bridges found in Suzhou and other cities in the Jiangnan region, the Wuting (Five Pavilions) Bridge in Yangzhou is a showy, stylish, and novel composition that is unrivaled in China. From some angles the bridge looks like a waterside building but from others it clearly serves as a bridge to allow both foot and boat traffic. Built in 1757 across a narrow inlet in Slender West Lake in Yangzhou to the back of the Lianxing Temple, the Wuting (Five Pavilions) Bridge was formally called the Lianhua (Lotus Flower) Bridge because of its resemblance to the open spreading petals of the flower.

Yangzhou, once one of the great cosmopolitan cities of late imperial China, is neither appreciated nor visited today in the ways it once was. Indeed, it was in Yangzhou that Marco Polo claimed to serve as governor for three years in the latter part of the thirteenth century. Located on the left bank of the Grand Canal a few miles north of the Chang Jiang (Yangzi River), the city prospered during the Qing dynasty because of its primacy in the national monopoly salt trade. During the eighteenth century especially—a time known for conspicuous consumption, extravagant displays of wealth, as well as creative construction—wealthy merchants, unconventional artists, and literary scholars brought about a transformation of the walled city's cultural landscapes. Here, stimulated by several inspection visits by the Qianlong emperor, a radical transformation of the city's landscapes emerged that displayed new tastes and innovative structures. Special attention was paid to building gardens of different sizes, including manipulating water bodies, piling up rocks, clustering vegetation, and inserting structures on and around them in order to heighten desired aesthetic effects. It was in this context that the space known as Slender West Lake, within which the rather eccentric Wuting or Five Pavilions Bridge was built, took shape as a component of a crafted landscape picture.

The base of the stone bridge has an overall length of 55.3 meters and rises about 8 meters above the water. Set upon twelve piers of varying sizes, the bridge

Right:
Viewed from this angle along the shoreline are five golden roofed pavilions, which collectively give the structure its name. The arches beneath and the stepped approaches on both sides affirm its function as a bridge that facilitates both foot and boat traffic.

Above:
The lotus leaves and flowers in the foreground highlight the approach to the steps leading upward into what appears like a waterside pavilion to those who do not know the structure serves also as a bridge.

Far left:
The alternating triangular drip tiles and circular drain tiles are all made of glazed ceramic and are imperial yellow in color.

Left:
The original stone carved lions found along the balustrades have weathered badly over the years to the degree that the detailed features on most have been obscured.

incorporates thirteen hemispheric arches as well as a pair of arch fragments set beneath the stairs that rise to five square, open-sided pavilions atop its base. Adjacent to the four enclosing single-eaved structures, the main central pavilion has a double-eaved roof that rises above it. Supported by slender scarlet pillars, each of the roofs of the symmetrical cluster of pavilions has an imperial yellow-tiled roof above it. While threaded through the center of the pavilions is a linking corridor connecting the stairs, the presence of low benches along the sides encourages visitors to linger and not simply transit the structure. Taken together, this bridge serves less as a means of passage than as a scenic spot to enjoy the surrounding mix of hills, vegetation, water, and boat traffic.

Other smaller bridges dot the shores of Slender West Lake, actually a natural waterway feeding mountain runoff into the Grand Canal, which is no longer a restricted precinct but a public park. Most notable is the Bridge of the Twenty-four, much heralded by Chinese scholars and the first to be built in the Sui dynasty during the sixth century. Here, it is said that twenty-four concubines played bamboo flutes to entertain a visiting emperor. The bridge itself has a unique 24-meter-long crescent shape, somewhat related to the Jade Belt Bridge in Beijing's Summer Palace. The bridge seen today was rebuilt in 1990.

During the first quarter of the nineteenth century, the gardens of Yangzhou became increasingly neglected and dilapidated as the gracious city generally entered a

Above:
The doubled upturned eaves and the curvature of the roof demanded complex carpentry in the construction of the covered bridge.

Left:
Each of the structural elements making up the five pavilions of the bridge includes elements common to any Chinese building: columns, posts, beams, rafters, ornamented panels, as well as a horizontal board declaring its poetic name, Lianhua (Lotus Flower) Bridge.

period of decline. Along Slender West Lake, the scene was described as a "yardful of broken pottery." The city was subsequently devastated during the depredations associated with the Taiping Rebellion in the mid-nineteenth century—as it had been earlier when the Manchus defeated the Ming imperial armies. Indeed, all of the roofed structures above the stone base of the Five Pavilions Bridge were burned, as were other buildings throughout the city. During the waning years of the Qing dynasty, and again in 1933, as well as between 1951 and 1953, attempts were made to restore the bridge structure to its earlier magnificence.

As a result of these various impacts over the past century and a half, Yangzhou as a city has been eclipsed by cities elsewhere in the region that rose to meet new commercial needs or were able to substantially restore the faded landscapes of their glorious pasts. Though less familiar than Hangzhou or Suzhou, Yangzhou once was known as a charming place in which great wealth accumulated and high culture flourished. Today, while transportation to Yangzhou is somewhat inconvenient, the well-planned city is worth a visit to see its restored waterways, gardens, and associated bridges as well as to search for opportunities to savor its literati cultural past. Flower festivals have an impressive history in Yangzhou, and it is in such places as Slender West Lake that one can enjoy the cultivated lakeside scenery of another time—including bridges—and today's periodic flower festivals while being sculled across the water in painted barques.

Above left and right:
Designed to provide a stroller with ever-changing perspectives, this zigzag bridge spans a narrow neck of water. The open shapes of butterflies have the symbolic meaning of "good fortune" because of a homophonous association.

Right:
First built during the Sui dynasty and rebuilt in its present form in 1990, the Bridge of the Twenty-four celebrates twenty-four concubines who played bamboo flutes to entertain a visiting emperor. Each side of the bridge has twenty-four marble steps and there are also twenty-four posts along the flanking balustrades. Moreover, its length is 24 meters and its width 2.4 meters. The bridge is part of a panoramic vista that incorporates a distant pagoda and a lakeside pavilion, with trees behind that obscure nearby buildings.

BAODAI BRIDGE

SUZHOU, JIANGSU

The multiple-span stone arch Baodai (Precious Belt) Bridge, constructed some 7 kilometers southeast of Suzhou city in Wuxian, is the oldest bridge still standing in Jiangsu province. Well known and appreciated by engineers and historians, the elegantly symmetrical bridge today nonetheless rests rather forlorn and forgotten amidst new highway construction and modernized canal traffic that mask its significant history and ingenious construction.

Built in the early ninth century during the Tang dynasty, along the line of several precursors, this stone bridge with replicated semicircular arches periodically underwent later unspecified modifications until about 1446 during the Ming dynasty when its current form was completed. The Tang Governor Wang Zhongshu, according to tradition, sold the precious belt given to him by the emperor to make up a shortfall in funds required to complete the bridge. As a result, the elongated silhouette, with its rising series of three middle arches, is said to be a reference to the shape of official Wang's jade belt floating on the water, in that Chinese belts of the

Below:
Stretching some 317 meters from shore to shore, the Baodai (Precious Belt) Bridge incorporates fifty-three arches that allow water from the adjacent Grand Canal and Dantai Lake to mix. The three elevated middle openings are said to resemble the shape of the buckle on an imperial official's jade belt.

time were broad, included multiple holsters for seals and other paraphernalia, and usually included a protruding buckle made of a precious stone or gold.

The Baodai Bridge, actually a continuation of the shoreline along the western side of the Grand Canal, a link in a canalside towpath which otherwise would have been broken because of the confluence of the two water bodies, spans an arm of the Dantai Lake as it empties into the Grand Canal. Its resourceful construction, with repeating arched openings, allows lake water and canal water to mix freely, a

condition that would have been impossible had a causeway-like embankment been built instead. The towpath function was only necessary at various times during the year when strong winds made it difficult for canal boats to move forward under sail.

With a consistent width of 4 meters after somewhat broader approaches and the absence of even a simple railing, the bridge-like towpath extends 317 meters from shore to shore. In addition to abutments that jut out from the shore, fifty-three arches continue to cross open water for some 250 meters. While

Top:
Carved from stone, this pair of lions stands guard at one entry to the Baodai Bridge. The male lion on the right can be identified since it has its right paw on a ball while the female has a cub under her left paw.

Above:
Strewn among the wildflowers and grass are Buddhist stupas and open structures covering stelae commemorating the building and repair of the Baodai Bridge.

fifty of the series of spans have openings of about 4 meters, three taller and broader arches along the northern half were raised to facilitate normal boat traffic between the canal and lake. The middle arch of these three reaches 6.95 meters with the two smaller ones 6 meters, rising together like a buckle on the flattened belt. Each of the arches is formed by thin piers only 0.6 meters in width set upon a base of wooden pilings and foundation stones that mitigate the instability of the subsoils where the waters mix. It is the multiple thin piers, each of which is remarkably flexible, combined with its low-lying extent that summons up the elegance to what is fundamentally a functional structure made of stone.

Although the bridge itself lacks applied or integrated ornamentation, at both ends are found a pair of carved stone protective lions. Midway along the bridge and at the northern terminus are similar 4.5-meter stone pagodas. The one in the north probably dates from the Southern Song period but the other is a modern reproduction. Buddha figures are carved on its five rising registers. Pagodas on bridges, like those situated on hilltops, served *fengshui* purposes in that they were expected to offer protection from malignant spirits as well as foul weather. Near the landed pagoda on the northern terminus is a small stone pavilion—a piece of architecture in stone—that covers a stele with inscriptions relating to the building and repair of the bridge. The 1874 stele, which has

substantial details about why repairs were necessary, ends with the invocation, "May this work be kept from decay so long as to become a Blessing for a hundred ages." Near by is a modern version of a God of War temple, still maintained by elderly ladies, that mimics one that once stood as a place of solace for trackers who passed in large numbers.

A feature of multi-span bridges with thin piers like the Baodai Bridge is that horizontal thrusts tend to balance each other, so shifting dead loads create only slight deformation in the shape of the piers and arches. Yet, as was witnessed in 1863 during fierce warfare that raged in the Jiangnan region during the Taiping Rebellion, the loss of a single span has a sequential effect that can potentially be cataclysmic.

The Englishman Charles Gordon, referred to often as "Chinese Gordon" since he commanded the fabled Ever-Victorious Army, a Qing-dynasty force comprising Chinese as well as foreigners to combat the Taiping rebels, ordered that the ninth arch of the Baodai Bridge be removed to permit his vessel to pass. His notes recall: "I am sorry to say that twenty-six of the arches fell in yesterday like a pack of cards, killing two men; ten others escaped by running, as the arches fell one after another, as fast as a man could run. It made a tremendous noise, and my boat was nearly smashed by the ruins. I regret it immensely, as it was unique and very old; in fact a thing to come some distance to see" (Hake, 1884: 78). Chinese

engineers note that the builders of the Baodai Bridge inserted a "brake pier," a larger pier than those adjacent, whose function was to offset lateral thrust and retard the full serial collapse of all the arches. The twenty-seventh pier from the northern end served this function well by limiting the complete destruction of the bridge by Gordon's necessary, but seemingly inconsequential, yet destructive action.

As a result of the collapse of nearly half of the arches, the bridge was rebuilt in 1872 in order to restore a critically needed tracking route along the Grand Canal. In 1937, the Japanese bombed six of the southern arches in an attempt to thwart commerce along the canal. Restoration work was not started until 1956, with full restoration completed only in 1983. But by then, trackers were no longer assisting canal barge traffic so the bridge no longer served its original function. What remains is a conspicuously elegant reminder of a utilitarian structure once critical in north–south commerce via the celebrated Grand Canal. On the fifteenth day of the eighth month of the lunar calendar during the Mid-Autumn Festival, local folks, as they have for centuries, still line the Baodai Bridge to view the moon when it is at its brightest and fullest. At the temple, they light incense and burn paper money in enormous censors to convey hopes for themselves and the maintenance of the bridge. Very few of them pay any attention to what was once an important landmark in the Jiangnan region.

Above:
The bulkiness of the stone approaches and stone arches of the Baodai Bridge contrast with the surrounding modern construction.

Left:
At a width of approximately 4 meters and without side railings, the Baodai Bridge clearly serves as an elegant towpath connecting two spits of land. A *samsara* stone is visible at the top of the raised central arch.

Below:
Close-up of the *samsara* stone, which represents the Buddhist belief in the endless round of birth, death, and rebirth.

HUIZHOU COVERED BRIDGES

ANHUI AND JIANGXI

With its sprawling mountains and dense system of rivers, the region in the southeast of China historically known as Huizhou was surprisingly both isolated and poor as well as accessible and cosmopolitan. Dominated by the lofty Huangshan or Yellow Mountains and divided by countless hillslopes, the region boasted hundreds of remote, relatively self-sufficient villages until its transformation began during the Song dynasty (960–1279) with the emergence of a distinctive mercantile system as the Southern Song capital moved to the city of Hangzhou in the Yangzi River delta, the capital of Zhejiang province and one of the most renowned and prosperous cities of China for much of the last 1,000 years.

Utilizing the prolific system of mountain-fed tributaries that ran into the Xin'an River, *keshang* or "traveling merchants" from Huizhou spread themselves widely, not only in Hangzhou but also into China's other great metropolitan centers in the Jiangnan region in the lower portions of the Yangzi River. Here, they amassed wealth from trade and pawnshops, sometimes even purchasing official titles that made it possible to improve their social status

Above:
With its roof lifted by timber pillars and beams and built much wider than a normal bridge, the capacious structure of the Tangmo Covered Bridge provides sufficient space for a performance stage as well as many tables for patrons to enjoy tea and local snacks.

Right:
Built between 1723 and 1735 and restored in 1996, the Tangmo Covered Bridge is a double-arch stone structure that spans a narrow stream, serving both as a passageway and a teahouse.

Top:
The Huanxiu Bridge appears now to be a small covered bridge, but actually is what remains of a longer five-span structure built during the Yuan dynasty (1279–1368). It once crossed a broad stream that has been narrowed by infilling.

Above:
Old worn wooden members have been supplemented with newer pieces to maintain the structural integrity of what is clearly a fragile bridge but one still used throughout the day by the elderly who come to sit and chat.

by becoming gentry-literati. Long-distance trade, first in timber, tea, lacquer, and especially salt, then later including the "four treasures of the scholar's studio"—paper, writing brushes, ink sticks, and ink slabs used by calligraphers—came to represent significant commercial resources for a distinctive and much-heralded group called Huizhou merchants.

The streamside pathway that leads into Tangmo village, Qiankou township, brings one quickly to an exceptional covered bridge built between 1723 and 1735 and restored in 1996. The bridge, straddling the tightly constricted stream that threads its way through the village, is a double-arch stone structure topped with a compact five-*jian* building that is able to function as both a teahouse and a performance stage because of its width.

Among the smallest covered bridges in Huizhou is the Huanxiu Bridge in Chengkan village, Huizhou district. While today but a modest intimation of what it once was, the bridge reveals a layered history. Built during the Yuan dynasty (1279–1368) by the widow of a young traveling merchant to memorialize him, the original bridge had five spans, each comprised of several cantilevered stone planks. During the Qing dynasty, a member of the dominant Luo lineage built a structure across the multiple spans for villagers to use as a place to relax. Over time, as the broad stream was filled in, only two spans remained, only one of which retains its austere shaded gallery. Still, throughout most of the day, the well-worn benches provide seats for grandparents to chat as they watch their grandchildren.

The humble Zhongshu Bridge in Likeng village in Wuyuan county, which today is part of Jiangxi province although historically a district in Huizhou, was built during the later part of the Northern Song dynasty by a *keshang* villager named Li Kan. It is said that Li Kan built the covered bridge in order to provide a resting place for villagers who had been using a simple log beam bridge as they traversed the fields. The covered bridge seen today, only 4 meters long and 2.5 meters wide, sits lightly atop a massive brick arched structure across a narrow watercourse. In many ways, the Zhongshu Bridge and nearly a dozen other small bridges in Liken are analogous to roadside pavilions called *lu ting*—some square, others rectangular, but all distinct—that provide similar resting opportunities for villagers throughout the built landscape of rural southern China.

Relatively unknown until recent times, the architectural heritage of Huizhou merchants is usually defined in terms of residences, ancestral temples, and academies—all rather similar in style because of their whitewashed walls and gray tiles—as well as imposing stone memorial archways called *paifang* and *pailou*. Yet, tucked within some of the old villages of Huizhou are bridges of great distinction, not only broad ones with multiple arches but also covered bridges of many sizes. Many of these bridges are mirrored in roadside pavilions, whose structure and purpose are similar, even though they do not cross water. While constructing residences clearly epitomizes their concern for the families they left behind

and their own hopes for a retirement sanctuary later in old age, it was through the building of schools, byways, roadside pavilions, and bridges that their civic consciousness was best shown. Family genealogies, which outline the history of a lineage in terms of birth and death records of all its members, also detail acts of public philanthropy such as the construction of bridges and roadside pavilions. While details of such charity may no longer be remembered clearly by most of the villagers, the presence of a covered bridge or pavilion is often accompanied by stone stelae that record details of its initial construction in addition to a listing of those who contributed towards its periodic restoration.

Above:
Throughout the Huizhou region, roadside pavilions and covered bridge pavilions were once quite common. The Zhongshu Bridge is along the path leading through a ceremonial gate, a *pailou*, to the village beyond.

Far left:
The complex carpentry of the Zhongshu's roof is seen in this view of splayed wooden rafters on which thin boards are laid to support the clay roof tiles.

Center:
The upturned eaves and end tiles of the Zhongshu Bridge all have subdued ornamentation.

Left:
Viewed from another angle, the Zhongshu Bridge looks more like a countryside pavilion than a serviceable structure—a comfortable space in which to sit, relax, and enjoy the surrounding scenery.

CAIHONG BRIDGE
WUYUAN, JIANGXI

No bridge is promoted more in Huizhou than the Caihong (Rainbow) Bridge in Qinghua township, Wuyuan county. Although called a "rainbow," the bridge neither soars nor is it arched; indeed, it is described as resting like a rainbow across the water. While overly touted as China's "most beautiful covered bridge," Caihong Bridge does have a charm derived more from its setting than its own character. Said to have been build some 800 years ago during the Southern Song dynasty, with a length of 140 meters and width of nearly 7 meters—the longest covered bridge in Huizhou—it is nonetheless an

Above:
The 140-meter-long Caihong (Rainbow) Bridge is used every day by villagers going back and forth to their fields.

Right:
Viewed from upstream, the Caihong Bridge is lifted by massive cut-stone piers in the shape of a prow, the pointed forward part of a boat's hull, which is said to boost the flow-through capacity of flood waters.

Left:
On the village side, the Caihong Bridge shares space with a small shop. All of the timber members of the bridge are purely functional pieces without distinction.

Below left:
As with more illustrious locations, Wuyuan county similarly promotes its "famous eight scenes," including the Caihong Bridge.

Opposite above:
The stone piers, viewed from downstream, provide substantial bases for the expansion of the corridor, spaces used for altars as well as relaxation.

Right:
While the actual corridor of the bridge is rather narrow, the space is broadened to nearly 7 meters on the downstream side above each of the piers, providing ample space for sitting as well as ritual at the shrines.

Far right:
The approach to the bridge from the nearby fields is via an inclined stone-paved path.

Left and right:
The mortise-and-tenoned joinery includes pegs that help hold the joints secure. Looking upwards towards the structural supports for the roof, it is obvious that the hewn and sawn timbers are only of modest dimensions.

important old structure. Four midstream boat-shaped piers and a pair of substantial abutments on both ends, all made of cut stone, support the wooden corridor bridge above. While the rear of each boat-shaped pier is square, like the stern of a skiff, the upstream end is pointed in shape, like a prow—referred to locally as a "swallow's beak"—a shape that is said to boost flow-through during seasonal flooding. Flow-through is also facilitated by the greater distance between the middle set of piers than the openings at the ends, the distance varying between 9.8 and 12.8 meters. The visual rhythm of the long covered wooden framework corridor fluctuates in both elevation and plan as the wooden structure widens and is elevated above each pier, permitting surprisingly broad spaces for each of the open pavilions.

Above the midway pier, a masonry building furnished with tables and benches made of cut stone also houses an elaborate shrine with a statue of Yu the Great, the tamer of floods. While the underlying masonry work is finely done, the carpentry above, while functional, is rather rudimentary, even crude.

Today, the Rainbow Bridge is the anchor for a scenic area set in the middle of an active village. Here, farmers go about their lives, including passing back and forth across the bridge, as tourists stop to capture images with their cameras of antique farm equipment as well as rural life that is slowly being transformed by their presence.

BEI'AN BRIDGE
SHEXIAN, ANHUI

Among the most substantial covered bridges in China, 33 meters long and 4.7 meters wide, is the Bei'an (Northern Stream) Bridge that crosses the Mian Stream in Shexian county. Built in the middle years of the Ming dynasty, with three stone arches and two midstream piers, this is the longest covered bridge in Huizhou. The covered portion, divided into eleven bays, consists of a wooden framework with solid walls of fired brick on both sides. Eight large square windows are cut into the east side, with eight others on the west wall in various auspicious shapes, including a full moon, flower pots, cassia leaves, and bottle gourds. Like many of China's larger

bridges, the Bei'an Bridge serves not only as a place to transit, a place to rest, but also as a location for a Buddhist shrine as well as a site for minor merchants to display what they have to sell to passersby.

Whether small or large, covered bridges in Huizhou are all relatively unassuming structures when compared to the magnificent corridor bridges of Guangxi, Fujian, and Zhejiang. None stand out because of sumptuous structures piled above them or are distinctive because of their innovative understructures. For the most part, they are merely serviceable in that they function as spans across waterways of various widths while providing spaces for villagers requiring a place to rest.

Right and below:
The covered masonry Bei'an Bridge is supported by three stone arches with two midstream piers. Eight large rectangular windows, each with a unique tracery pattern, are found on the east side. On the west side, in addition to a reclining seat that protrudes from the bridge, there are window openings in the shape of various auspicious Buddhist symbols.

Above:
The walls on the west side of the bridge are enhanced with eight windows in various auspicious shapes, including a full moon flanked on each side by a flower pot, a cassia leaf, and a bottle gourd. On the left is a projecting seating area with a roof overhang.

Right:
From the projecting seating area, a family is able to relax while enjoying the view of the village scenery beyond.

Top:
Both ends of the bridge have a tunnel-like entry.

Above:
Shaped like a bottle gourd, this aperture in the masonry wall on the west side of the Bei'an Bridge frames part of the village landscape.

Left:
Divided into eleven bays, the covered corridor consists of a wooden framework lifting the roof. Solid walls of fired brick are laid between the columns on both sides.

MEGALITHIC STONE BEAM BRIDGES

QUANZHOU, FUJIAN

For nearly 700 years from the sixth century onwards—from the Tang through the Song dynasties—an extraordinary period of commercial development and trade brought the once-remote southeastern seacoast region into the imperial system. As part of this integration, especially during the middle two centuries of the Song dynasty (960–1279), megalithic stone beam bridges were built along the embayed shoreline of Fujian, a province noted for narrow coastal plains tucked into an indented rugged coastline that frustrated overland travel. Throughout the province, short rivers pour out of the nearby mountains where they disgorge into broad tidal inlets that created extraordinary challenges to any efforts to span them with structures of any type, let alone utilizing megaliths that are unique in the world.

Megalithic bridges in Fujian, as with bridges of other types elsewhere in China, were constructed under the supervision of local prefects as well as Buddhist monks who gained merit from building what were clearly structures of extraordinary length and dimensions. Much remains obscure about the origins and construction methods of these massive bridges, but remnants suggest remarkably practical engineering skills that made it possible to maneuver stone slabs

Below and right:
Built in the middle of the twelfth century to cross a shallow estuary, the Anping Bridge, with a length of 2.07 kilometers supported by 331 piers, deserves its historical accolade, "no bridge under the sun is as long as this one." Today, the bridge provides a quiet route for lovers, bikers, and hikers, who find that its location affords tranquility and a good breeze.

that reached 20 meters in length and 200 metric tons in weight. A seventeenth-century drawing reveals the use of shear-legs derricks in hoisting massive stone slabs during a period of repair. According to various records, in a relatively brief thirty-year period alone, giant stone beam bridges totaling 15 kilometers were constructed throughout Fujian.

Galeote Pereira, the first Westerner to write of these bridges, made the following observations at the end of the sixteenth century: "The breadth of the bridges, although it be well proportioned unto the length thereof, yet they are equally buylt, no higher in

Above:
This early woodblock print map of Quanzhou shows not only the irregularly circular city wall but also the moat, sea, and embayed coastline that frustrated overland travel.

the middle than at eyther end, in such wuse that you may directly see from the one end to the other; and the sydes are wonderfully well engraved after the manner of Rome workes. But that wee did most marveyle at, was therwithall the hugeness of the stones…. I have been astunned to behold the hugeness of these aforesaid stones, some of them are xii pases long and upwarde, the least a good xi pases long, and a halfe" (quoted in Boxer, 1953: 7).

It is likely that Pereira was commenting on either the Luoyang Bridge, also called the Wan'an Bridge, or the Anping (Peace) Bridge, the most striking megalithic bridges found near the center of maritime trade, the important seaport of Quanzhou. Before these bridges were built, travelers had to spend days walking inland in order to get from one side of a bay to the other or, alternatively, chance drowning if taking a small craft across the shifting mudflats of the tidal inlet. These two bridges, as well as others to the north and south, were part of an extensive developing road network that linked southeastern China first with Kaifeng, the imperial capital in the Huang He Valley in the north, and later the Southern Song capital of Hangzhou in neighboring Zhejiang. Products as varied as dried powdered tea, fruits, and ceramics became staples moved via the trade networks.

The Luoyang Bridge, begun about 1053 and completed in six years, provided a safe alternative to a dangerous ferry and later a pontoon bridge that had been incapable of meeting commercial needs. Built in an area where the Luoyang River turbulently meets the tidal surge of the sea 13 kilometers to the northeast of Quanzhou, a foundation of stone blocks—an underwater stone causeway running the length of the bridge from shore to shore—provided the base for the boat-shaped stone piers that depended upon their sheer

weight to support the bridge and to survive the movement of the tides. Much of the original base remains, but since the early 1930s a reinforced concrete pavement spans the water, and in the decade after 1991 extensive work has further restored this important bridge. With forty-seven spans and an overall length of 1100 meters and a width of 4.5 meters, the bridge, according to local legend, was built with the aid of

Left:
Found etched on an old, undated stone tablet, this is the earliest extant record of the Luoyang Bridge. Only one enclosed resting place of the thirty-seven once extant, perhaps some of which also were shrines, is shown on the right.

Chinese engineers point to the ingenious use of living oysters to anchor the stone foundations upon which the piers were set. Today, the cultivation of oysters in the mudflats adjacent to the bridge hints at the possibility of their use as an organic mastic since the larvae cement themselves to rocks, shells, or any other solid objects, spending their lives secure in one place while opening their growing shells to filter algae from the water. Taking advantage of a principle of biologic engineering, oysters could be placed within crevices in the stone, fastening themselves securely, and then growing in a way that would stabilize the structure.

While there is a record of a 6000-meter-long stone beam bridge with some 23 larger and 140 smaller spans built in 1154, common lore in Fujian heralds the Anping (Peace) Bridge, built between 1138 and 1151, with the appellation "no bridge under the sun is as long as this one." Located some 30 kilometers southwest of Quanzhou, between Jinjiang and Nanan, the bridge crosses an arm of the sea with a length of 2070 meters, more than 2 kilometers, supported by 331 piers that vary in shape depending on the depth and movement of the water. Most piers are rectangular where they rise only a short distance above shallow water. Where water is deep on one side and shallow on the other, the shape is flat on one end and pointed on the other. Twenty-seven of the piers are like the pointed ones on both ends on the Luoyang Bridge. Portions of the Anping Bridge are sometimes submerged, depending on the height of the tides, and some adjacent areas have been filled in with silt where once tidal waters flowed freely. Six to seven slabs 8–10 meters long, with gaps between them, span pairs of piers. Five pavilions were once placed along the lengthy bridge for the use of passersby in need of rest or protection from the

various immortals who fitted into place the 11-meter-long granite slabs forming the deck. Some of these slabs weighed as much as 150 metric tons and were positioned using the ebb and flow of the tides. Today, what remains is a substantial fragment of its original form: some 800 meters of the bridge's original 1100 meter length, thirty-one of forty-seven piers, one of seven pavilions, and three of nine votive stupas.

Below:
Dated 1690, this rare woodblock print portrays the use of a shear-legs derrick to lift and position the megalithic stones employed in the construction or reconstruction of the Luoyang Bridge. The larger buildings may be shacks for workers or shelter for equipment. The depiction of the bridge is, in fact, secondary to what is depicted in the foreground, the martial activities of General Wu, a Qing dynasty commander.

Above:
Facing upstream along the Luoyang Bridge, this carved face of a protective Bodhisattva graces one side of a stupa that has Buddhist prayers and small images of the Buddha carved around the other sides.

Far left:
This is one of at least a dozen stone stupas that remain at either end of the Luoyang Bridge. It is not clear how many have been lost over the centuries or the specific reasons why each was placed.

Left:
These women are returning home with baskets filled with oysters that had just been harvested from the mudflats beneath the Luoyang Bridge as the tide receded.

elements. Near the center of the Anping Bridge is an island with a tranquil temple

Over time, some spans of these megalithic bridges collapsed as their piers subsided or the tensile strength of a stone beam was exceeded, leading to fracture. In other cases, the scouring effect of currents and tides, coupled with the substantial dead load of the granite, shifted piers and led to shearing. Since repairs often were not made with stone of the same dimensions, piers and beams came to vary significantly. Moreover, repairs sometimes necessitated cantilevering and mismatched stacking. Sometimes, a new pier had to be placed between a pair of old ones to accommodate replacement stone and, in recent times, even concrete beams have been used. Thus, the original appearance of many bridges underwent significant modification. From time to time, a bridge had to be abandoned, leaving only clustered fragments of rubble in the mud.

The Buddhist influence on the Luoyang and Anping megalithic bridges can be glimpsed from the abundance of auspicious imagery, statues, steles, votive stupas, as well as statues of lions in addition to generals and officials that populate the otherwise rather stark structures. Not too far from the northern end of the Luoyang Bridge is the small but active Zhaohui Temple and a shrine, while on the southern end is a hall commemorating Cai Xiang, the official credited with overseeing its construction. On an island midway across the Anping

Bridge as well as at one end, there are larger temples. Except for Buddhist iconography, these bridges are generally rather plain, with only their stark flat lines and textured stone surfaces offering any aesthetic qualities. For the most part, the megalithic stone beam bridges are functional spans that give evidence of the Song bridge builders' complete mastery of complex technical and logistical skills.

Elsewhere in the world, of course, mysteries still remain as to how even prehistoric builders were able to maneuver massive stones and roughly hewn stone slabs to create megalithic monuments for funerary and religious purposes. Yet, whether prehistoric monument or structures built on solid ground, the technical tasks of successfully manipulating massive blocks of dressed granite stone and placing them on and above shifting tidal flats of the Fujian littoral was a greater technical challenge. Fujian builders no doubt drew from their long experience in utilizing stone hewn from extensive quarries in the nearby mountains as building material for constructing stone houses, stone dykes, and stone seawalls, as well as making stone coffins. Even today, the ubiquity of stone in Fujian construction far exceeds that found elsewhere in China. Hauling stone great distances seems never to have been difficult; the challenge was manipulating stone over water because the density of the granite obviously far exceeded that of the water.

Top:
The very old trees, stupas, and small structures suggest that the western end of the Luoyang Bridge once had temples, as are still found on the opposite end. However, today the buildings merely shelter old stone tablets and provide storage.

Above:
This close-up view of one of the stone cutwaters extending out from a pier shows the ingeniously strong configuration used, held in place with at least one metal key.

COVERED WOODEN BRIDGES

SOUTHERN ZHEJIANG AND NORTHERN FUJIAN

While news of the existence of wooden covered "rainbow bridges"—ingenious soaring arches built using technologies thought lost in the twelfth century—began to emerge in the writings of a few specialists in the 1970s, the bridges remained essentially "unknown" to outsiders until the very end of the twentieth century. Over the past decade, however, more than a hundred of these extraordinary bridges have been slowly "discovered," visited, described, and photographed, revealing in the process an extent that could not have been anticipated by those who saw the handful of earliest examples of "rainbow bridges" some thirty years ago. How could a distinctive structural form, once apparently common, ostensibly die out? How could such a form not only be preserved in a remote mountain region but also continue to be built in the middle of the twentieth century? More than a hundred known bridges of this type are found in contiguous counties in both northern Fujian (Shouning, Fu'an, and Nanping) and southern Zhejiang (Taishun, Qingyuan, Yunhe, and Jingning), just 10 percent of those recorded in the nineteenth century. Moreover, it is likely that other examples remain undiscovered in remote mountain areas. How these bridges fitted into the centuries-old transportation network has yet to be teased out.

In Zhejiang's remote mountainous Taishun county, 958 bridges of various types were counted in 1987. These included rather simple block stone bridges as well as more sophisticated stone beam bridges, stone arch bridges, timber beam bridges, and what were being called timber arch bridges. While stone beam bridges and stone arch bridges are the most widespread types found in this region, timber beam and timber arch structures are numerous and truly outstanding. Considered true "rainbow bridges," this last type indeed comprises matchless structures employing engineering principals believed to have died out in China some 900 years ago, and, somewhat surprising, seen nowhere else in the world.

Left:
Initially built in 1741 and reconstructed many times since, the Yangmeizhou Bridge soars with a span of 35.7 meters above the streambed of a deep valley in Shouning county, Fujian.

Right:
The Xuezhai Bridge in Taishun county, Zhejiang, was first built in 1512 and then rebuilt in 1857. It connects two parts of a town, serving as a space for relaxation as well as for peddlers to sell goods.

Throughout the mountainous area, bridge structures of all four types are often capped with wooden buildings that transform the spans into *covered* bridges quite unlike those found in North America and Europe. Some covered bridges here are relatively level structures with gradual approaches, just as they are typically found elsewhere in the world, while many rear up abruptly from their abutments and soar dramatically as they cross over steep chasms. Local people refer to these dramatically ascending types as

"centipede bridges" because of their resemblance to the arch-like rise of a long arthropod's body as it crawls.

In actual fact, none of the covered structures, which appear from a distance to be supported by a wooden arch, is actually atop an actual arch. Rather, the illusionary "arch" emerges from using a series of logs, long tree trunks gathered from the nearby forests, that function as interwoven chords or segments of the "arch." Chinese engineers, such as the well-regarded Mao Yisheng and Tang Huangcheng,

Above:
When approached from the paths on the flanks of the adjacent hillslopes, the profile of the Xianju Bridge in Taishun county, Zhejiang, is said by local residents to appear like a crawling centipede.

refer to the structure of such bridges as being a "woven timber arch," or "combined beam timber-arch," or "interlocked timber arch" to underscore the use of straight timber members tied together. Yang Hongxun, an architectural historian, suggests combining the terms so that the nomenclature becomes "woven beam timber arch," which aligns it with technological descriptions already accepted among Chinese architectural historians who examine other structures, such as palaces, temples, and dwellings.

The basic components of rainbow bridges are quite simple: two pairs of two layered sets of inclined timbers, with each of the sets embedded in opposite abutments, stretch upward toward the middle of the stream. To fill the gap between these two inclined timber sets, a pair of horizontally trending assemblages of timbers is attached. Transverse timbers tenoned to them and/or tied with rattan or rope hold each of the sets of timbers together. It is these warp and weft elements that give rise to the term

Pages 222–3:
The Luanfeng (Mythical Bird Peak) Bridge, with a length of 47.7 meters and an open span of 37.9 meters—the broadest of any of China's extant woven timber frame bridges—can only be dated to 1800 although there is some evidence of a bridge existing at this site earlier. Xiadang township, Shouning county, Fujian.

"woven." X-braces are sometimes used to enhance structural strength. While the downward pressure of the weighty logs compresses all the components together into a tight and relatively stable composition, the equilibrium can sometimes be upset if forces from beneath—such as might come from torrential floods or typhoon winds—push upward.

Computer simulation analysis by Liu Jie and Shen Weiping revealed that this woven composition of logs operates like both an arch structure as well as a beam structure in the mechanical sense. Thus, the technical term describing the configuration, they suggest, is better called a "woven timber arch-beam" structure—with the word "beam" being added—to better describe mechanically its form. To further provide stability to the underlying "woven timber arch-beam" structure, additional weight is added by erecting a building on top of the bridge, thus creating a covered bridge. The heavy timber columns, beams, balustrades, and baked clay roof tiles, add substantial weight—a dead load—which somewhat counter intuitively enhances stability, reducing possible damage from both torrential flash floods and typhoon winds. With the addition of wooden skirts along the side perimeter, moreover, the wooden members of the bridge are also protected from weathering and deterioration.

While "woven timber arch-beam" rainbow bridges in Zhejiang and Fujian are similar to each other, there are many minor variations, which may have resulted from trial and error—creative mutations—arising from local circumstances. Four bridges—three in Taishun county, Zhejiang; two in Qingyuan county, Zhejiang; and one in Pingnan county, Fujian—illustrate these similarities and differences.

Aside from looking at the structure of the Fujian-Zhejiang rainbow bridges, it is important to realize as well that the covered bridges serve as multifunctional sites for a variety of activities: a place to rest for travelers, itinerants, and workers; a place for women to make handicrafts and watch over their children; a place to make offerings and pray; as well as a site to spread out goods to sell. Located at an elevated position in the midst of a gorge usually means that a breeze passes through the upper structure, with the result that bridges are always a cool place to sit and talk, or even spend the night.

As can be seen in other sections, the presence of small and large altars with all the accouterments of worship permit personal prayer as well as community ritual. Near towns, especially, the approaches to bridges provide sites for building shops that were easily accessible to those crossing the bridge. Liu Jie and a Chinese-American, Frank Shouzhang Ye, have suggested using the English words "lounge bridges" to describe these multiple functions and capture the similarity of sound with *langqiao*, the Chinese word used for "covered bridge."

The Carpenters

Although knowledge about the actual building of rainbow bridges in the past is still in its infancy, preliminary research points to the prominence of members of two families of master builders and apprentices, surnamed Xu and Zheng, in the construction of the bridges. These carpenter families built and repaired rainbow bridges for six generations, spanning 110 years, from the middle of the nineteenth century through the construction of the Red Army Bridge in 1954. It is also known that the father–son team of Zheng Huifu and Zheng Duojin constructed eighteen timber arches spread across mountainous territory in six counties, five of them in Taishun county, Zhejiang.

The memories of the now elderly son, Zheng Duojin, who was seventy-seven in 2006, reveals clearly the vagaries of bridge construction. Floods destroyed rainbow bridges built in 1948 and 1953. These were swept away by mountain torrents within a few years. Neither of these bridges was rebuilt. Whether the site was abandoned as unsatisfactory and wooden members collected and stored for use in repairs elsewhere, or moved to another site, such as the Red Army Bridge that was subsequently constructed is not clear. No doubt trial and error was a necessary approach to traditional bridge building, where circumstances changed and resources varied.

The modular character of Chinese construction using wooden members means that little is really lost when a building, such as a bridge, collapses. Throughout China today, it is possible to observe the scavenging of building materials when old dwellings and temples are dismantled. Timbers, tiles, stones, bricks, among other components, are always collected and stored for later use. The mind-set of carpenters is usually pragmatic as they modify components to meet new needs, with the result that variations on standard practices are usually observable. In fact, as can be seen in any of the bridges still standing throughout the region, new building members are regularly swapped for deteriorating ones. Timber in the mountains of Fujian and Zhejiang provides a rich resource for the building of bridges and dwellings.

Bridges and Byways

To focus only on the techniques of building bridges and their often astonishing beauty unintentionally obscures the fact that any single bridge in China is likely to be just one link in an extensive system of bridges, fords, and ferries that themselves are but elements of a wide-ranging network of roads, paths, and byways. While countless wooden bridges are still in existence in the mountainous areas of southern Zhejiang and northern Fujian provinces, this combined area seems also an improbable region to find an integrated traditional transportation network. Yet, the presence of so many extant old bridges, some of which are truly unique structures, and the traces of old paths among them, provide a framework for scholars to understand the emergence of a significant regional culture from the fourteenth through the nineteenth centuries in ways so easily studied elsewhere in China. Remote from major cities and cut off by precipitous cliffs and raging streams, this mountainous region—until quite recently—was seemingly isolated from economic development taking place elsewhere in coastal China.

Opposite:
The lofty Luanfeng Bridge in Shouning county, Fujian, was rebuilt in 1800 to replace a bridge whose origin is unclear. Rising high above the streambed, the bridge has a clear span of 37.6 meters, exceeding that of any other bridge of this type. The large boulders in the foreground have been carried to this location by floods that may have accompanied a typhoon.

Above left and below:
Interior details on covered bridges, such as ceilings and carvings, usually vary from bridge to bridge or within a single bridge, as shown here. Xidong Bridge, Taishun county, Zhejiang.

Above:
The highest portion of the corridor of the covered Xianju Bridge is level while on either side the wooden floor slopes down rather precipitously.

Santiao Bridge
Taishun, Zhejiang

Straddling a rock-strewn ravine between Zhouling and Yangxi townships, where four interprovincial mountain byways converge, the Santiao Bridge is the region's oldest rainbow bridge. Records indicate that there was a bridge here as early as the Tang dynasty, which was repaired in 1137 during the Song dynasty. The bridge seen today was built in 1843 and has undergone a series of renovations over the century and a half of its existence. The only access to the bridge is via the old stone-lined paths that drop out of the mountains to cross the gorge via the bridge. Rising an impressive height of about 10 meters above the bed of the stream, the bridge is 32 meters long with an open span of 21.26 meters, and has no supporting midway pier. The covered portion includes eleven bays with sawn timber cladding and a relatively simply two-slope tile roof. Transverse and longitudinal drawings of the bridge show clearly the relationship between the stone abutments—seven major and six minor logs—which are tied together by a pair of crosspieces and strengthened with an X-shaped brace to give strength to the "arch." Atop this structure are longitudinal members, which then are tied to the mortise-and-tenoned building above to form a covered arcade running from end to end. Because the location of the bridge is so well chosen,

there is no need to climb steps to cross it. The symmetrical bracket sets extend the eaves well beyond the vertical line of the bridge below. In conjunction with the wooden cladding, this substantial overhang helps protect the underlying wooden structure.

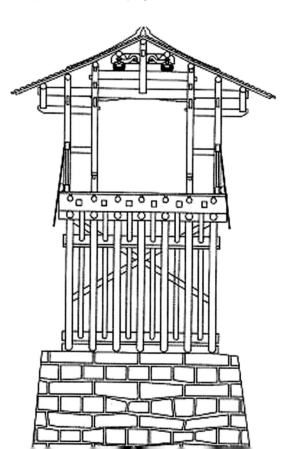

Above left and right:
Whether viewed from the boulder-strewn floor of the mountain stream or from any of the paths that drop from the surrounding mountains, the Santiao Bridge, the oldest of Taishun county's wooden rainbow bridges, occupies a beautiful site. Set deep in a V-shaped valley, the bridge was a critical link in a system of byways connecting southern Zhejiang and northern Fujian provinces. Records clearly show that there has been a bridge here since the Tang dynasty, and one can see nearby the hollowed-out sockets chiseled into the exposed stone outcrops that indicate the location of earlier bridges.

Left:
This transverse section perspective exposes the three components of the Santiao Bridge: a stone foundation, an assemblage of seven major and six minor logs that form the arches, and atop this a gallery made of a wooden pillar-and-tie beam framework.

Above:
The interlinked logs that allow the bridge to soar more than 21 meters across the valley bottom are clearly shown in this view from beneath.

Above right:
At the far end of the wooden corridor is a shrine that was moved outside during reno-vation in order to reduce the chance of fire.

Right:
This incense burner is located between the shrine and the bridge itself.

Pages 230–1:
The stone-lined paths on both sides of the Santiao Bridge attest to its importance as a strategic crossing point.

Xidong and Beijian Bridges
Taishun, Zhejiang

The Xidong Bridge and Beijian Bridge, a pair of nearby bridges, cross one of two streams in a town called Sixi. Built in 1570, refurbished in 1745, and taking its current form in 1827, the Xidong Bridge lays a bit closer to the water, with a length of 41.7 meters, a width of 4.86 meters, and a span of 25.7 meters. The Xidong Bridge is just 500 meters upstream from the Beijian Bridge, and is sometimes called a "sister" bridge. Built initially in 1674, rebuilt in 1849, and then again in 1987, the Beijian Bridge is 51.7 meters long and 5.37 meters wide, with a clear span of 29 meters. Although it rises some 11.22 meters above the streambed, which often has a sluggish watercourse passing under it, rushing torrents of water can bring seasonal flooding, as in September 2005 when flood waters submerged the abutments and wrecked considerable damage, but failed to sweep away the bridge.

Both bridges have external skirts made of sawn timber that disguise the underlying structure, giving

Above left:
Structural flourishes within the Xidong Bridge rise to support a winged bat, whose presence itself is more than ornamental since the bat is an auspicious creature. The Chinese word for

bat is homophonous with *fu*, meaning "good fortune."

Above right:
Much of the interior carpentry work goes beyond being mere function.

Above:
With its copious overhangs, upturned eaves, and external ornamentation, the Xidong Bridge once dominated its location. Today, the surrounding multistoried shops and homes have diminished its presence somewhat.

Left:
Rising more than 10 meters above a usually slow-moving stream, the Xidong Bridge is entered via stone steps that lead to an elaborate wooden gallery with a loft above its central bay, which houses an altar.

Above:
The Beijian Bridge is considered by many to be Taishun's most beautiful covered bridge. Although rising more than 11 meters above the water below and spanning 26 meters, the bridge nonetheless is periodically assaulted by rushing flood waters that surge upwards to lap its flanks.

Left:
Crowded with very old trees, the steps leading to the Beijian Bridge move from the river bottom to the security of an upland area.

Below:
While similar to other wooden framework corridors, that of the Beijian Bridge has more carved timber members and is wider and taller.

Opposite right:
The downward-hanging component at the junction of horizontal and vertical wooden parts near the main altar has been given a flourish.

Opposite far right:
The red line on the stone steps leading to the Beijian Bridge marks the height that the flood waters rose to on September 1, 2005, wrecking much damage.

the appearance that they are structurally built atop an arch formed by three timber chords. In fact, the "arch" is an illusion. When one looks up from under each bridge, each superstructure is seen clearly as a set of interwoven tree trunks. While differing in details, both include two pairs of double-layered inclined timbers, which are embedded in stone abutments. Since the sets of inclined timbers do not meet, another two sets of horizontally laid timbers are put between them. While tenon joinery and rattan rope play some role in tying the system together, it is the positioning and weight of the horizontal timbers that secure the structure. The addition of X-braces helps to further stabilize the "woven" nature of the interlocked system. Operating together, the timber components function like a stone arch in compression as forces push outward against the abutments.

The internal portions of the covered galleries of both bridges are similar although each has distinctive entryways. The Beijian Bridge is entered on one end via a series of steep steps that lead to a cluster of wooden shops that are tied to the bridge itself. The Xidong Bridge has a roadside entry that is somewhat like a porte-cochere, a portico-like structure. While the Beijian Bridge is somewhat longer, with nineteen modular bays compared to the Xidong Bridge with fifteen, both were built using pillars-and-transverse-tie beams mortised together. Each pillar is set atop a stone pedestal and rises to directly support a roof purlin. No groundsills tie adjacent frames of individual bays together, but the connecting wooden railings and benches serve as stabilizing components. Along both sides of the bridges, projecting tie beams, some tiered with supporting struts, elongate the structure beyond the side walls, in the process creating substantial curved eaves overhangs that shade the timbers beneath from rainfall. Within both bridges are intricate wooden alcoves containing images of local gods and goddesses.

Xuezhai Bridge
Taishun, Zhejiang

The impressive Xuezhai Bridge, named after the Xue family whose contributions and power led to its construction in 1857, is set up to link two sides of a stream in Sankui town, Taishun county. Along the immediate approach to the bridge, the stone stelae present facts concerning the building of the bridge and the generosity of individuals and families who funded its construction. However, it is left to local lore to reveal the complications and animosities that arose with both the building and renovation of the bridge. Records show that there was a precursor span called the Jinxi (Embroidered Stream) Bridge on this site from as early as 1512, and that flooding periodically led to damage and rebuilding amidst prolonged and recurring community tensions as well as philanthropic competition.

After a great flood in 1579, however, there were insufficient resources to rebuild and the town had to make do with a nearby smaller bridge. Meanwhile, the Zhang family purchased one bank of the stream on which the earlier bridge had been built, a location that was believed to have the attributes of the tortoise-snake, according to the canon of *fengshui*. When the Xu family decided in 1739 to build a Wugong or "centipede bridge," the local name for a soaring wooden covered bridge, the Zhang family objected because of the widespread belief that centipedes devour snakes and tortoises. If the Xue family succeeded, this would mean that the Zhang family would be diminished. As a result, it was not possible to build a centipede bridge until 1857, after the Xue family gained the support of all the other clans in the village and after the Zhang family had sold the land.

While the overall length of the bridge is 51 meters, the span is only 29 meters, which rises like a high arch some 10.5 meters above the creek below. The steep set of cut-stone steps leading to the bridge itself gives pedestrians the sense of crossing an arch-type bridge because of the dramatic rise, but a view from below shows that the underlying structure is a system of interlocked timbers. The massive stone abutments formed by the buttressing stairs take the lateral thrusts of the massive timber frame. As the illustrations reveal, the fifteen structural bays are quite simple and regular. With its upturned eaves, the roofline looks much like that of a country temple. In recent years, much repair work has been done on the bridge so that the modular nature of the wooden framework is quite apparent.

At one time, the soaring Xuezhai Bridge dominated its site, with only a large camphor tree beside it. Today, both are overwhelmed by drab, unfinished multistoried buildings that cluster around them and diminish the beauty of this community emblem.

Above right:
Once a bucolic scene, with only an ancient camphor tree growing out of the riverbank, the Xuezhai Bridge is now "lost" among dozens of looming multistoried brick and cement buildings.

Right:
Because the Xuzhai Bridge connects two areas of the town, the covered corridor sees much activity by pedestrians and those simply wanting to sit in a cool spot to rest or chat.

Left:
The short king post supporting the ridge beam is ornamented with several sym-
metrical wooden carvings.

Above:
The interdigitated parallel log assembly supporting the bridge includes horizontal members that help "lock" the timbers into secure positions.

Right:
The Rulong (Like a Dragon) Bridge in Qingyuan county, Zhejiang, is notable for its unusual three pavilion-like structures: a pavilion on the south end (left), with three entries from stone pathways; a cluster of altars in the center; and a three-tiered overhanging gabled structure on the north end (right), with two entries, that served as a bell tower.

Rulong Bridge
Qingyuan, Zhejiang

Qingyuan county claims a glorious history that dates back to the Song dynasty, a time in which the imperial family in Hangzhou reached into the mountains for exotic foods and medicines. In an area said to have "10 bridges in a distance of 1 *li*," the Rulong or Like a Dragon Bridge is an exceptional bridge in a township with many fine extant bridges. This covered bridge, which was located along a major trade route between Fujian to the south and the Jiangnan region to the north, however, was not built until the later part of the Ming dynasty, in 1625. The bridge has a clear span of 19.5 meters, a length of 28.2 meters, and a width of 5.09 meters, with nine interior modular bays. Its underlying support is very much like that of other "woven timber arch-beam" structures, with its distinction arising from the magnitude and extent of the covered portions above. In addition to a double layer of overlapping wooden skirts along the side and along

Left:
The dimensions of both the beams, shown here, and the columns supporting them are much greater than those on more common covered bridges, clearly attesting to the magnitude of the donations to build the bridge.

the beams, there are three pavilion-like structures that rise above the roof. On the north end is a three-tiered overhanging gabled structure that served as a bell tower, with two entries. On the south end is a pavilion with three entries from stone pathways. The central elevated structure houses a complex of altars. Being recognized for its significance, the Rulong Bridge was declared a National Historic Site in 2001.

Above:
Bracket sets of this complexity are very rare within wooden covered bridges. Here, however, they are used to lift the central pavilion roof above the altars in the central bay of the Rulong Bridge.

Right:
Since the restoration of the Rulong Bridge, no effort has been made to replace the images of deities that once populated the altar on the left. Above the empty *shenkan* is a horizontal board proclaiming the name of the bridge, above which is a coffered ceiling.

Wan'an Bridge
Pingnan, Fujian

Unlike soaring rainbow bridges, the Wan'an (Eternal Peace) Bridge in Fujian, which has a similar underlying structure, is noted more for its length. Crossing a broad river, the bridge today has an overall span of 98.2 meters while being only 8.5 meters above the water. Its dimensions have varied over

time as the bridge was damaged and then rebuilt. With such a long span and a covered structure that runs approximately 100 meters, it was necessary to have the support of five piers. Between the piers are six "woven timber arch-beam" structures that vary in their spans, the greatest being 15.3 meters and the smallest 10.6 meters. Although the bridge is level, one must climb thirty-six steps on the northwest end and ten steps on the southwest end to reach it.

Above:
With five stone piers, stone abutments on each end, and six sets of "woven timber arch-beam" supports, the Wan'an (Eternal Peace) Bridge in Fujian is the longest bridge of its type in China.

Incomplete records indicate that the Wan'an Bridge was destroyed many times over the years, more as a result of local conflicts than natural disasters. A bridge was built here first during the Song dynasty but was destroyed in 1648 during the turmoil of the transition from the Ming to the Qing dynasty, some say by bandits who made off with the wooden components. Although rebuilt in 1742 during the settled early years of the reign of the Qianlong emperor, a time of prosperity in China, it was put out of commission again twenty-five years later. While rebuilt in 1845, the bridge was consumed by fire in the early Republican period of the twentieth century. In 1932, when it was rebuilt, the overall structure was lengthened. Flood damage in 1952 destroyed nearly a third of the wooden structure, which led to reconstruction in 1954 in the form seen today.

Top:
With its curved back supports, the bench seating along the sides of the Wan'an Bridge provides comfort and community space for villagers.

Above:
The approach up steep cut-stone steps at each end of the Wan'an Bridge suggests one is entering a temple.

Houkeng Bridge
Qingyuan, Zhejiang

Houkeng Bridge is one of the thirteen surviving timber arched corridor bridges in Qingyuan county, Zhejiang. Originally built in 1671 and renovated a number of times over the centuries, the bridge nonetheless had fallen into substantial disrepair by the late 1980s. Because of rotting as well as the theft of some wooden structural parts, iron pipes had to be added to prop up the arch.

By 2001, when circumstances had become quite dire, significant efforts began to be expended to restore the bridge but these were initially frustrated because of the shortage of available funding. In reviewing possibilities, it was recollected that the bridge had played a role in a battle between Communist and Guomindang armies on August 30, 1934 and had been dubbed a "Red Army bridge" during the Great Proletarian Revolution in order to save it from wanton desecration. The desire to preserve a "Red" site rather than merely an old bridge quickly gained momentum under the slogan "Carry Forward the 'Red' Tradition, Promote the Redevelopment of Qingyuan."

The signs around the site today clearly demarcated the bridge's military significance, validating its recent importance, but with minimal acknowledgment of the Houkeng Bridge's significance as an engineering achievement. Indeed, the county's website proclaims that the bridge's name, "Red Army bridge," first surfaced soon after the 1934 battle nearby. Nonetheless, those involved in the dismantling and reconstruction of the bridge paid great attention to conservation principles, historically accurate rebuilding, and careful documentation of the process. Recognizing its importance, the Houkeng Bridge was nominated for an international award, and was granted a 2005 Award of Excellence in the UNESCO 2005 Asia-Pacific Heritage Awards for Culture Heritage Conservation competition. The press release highlighted "the community's respect for historic engineering principles" but did not mention the bridge's "Red" history.

Above right:
The Houkeng Bridge, originally built in 1671, was later christened a "Red Army bridge" because of a nearby battle. The bridge was restored beginning in 2001.

Right:
The careful restoration of the bridge's underlying interior wooden framing and timber arch-beam structure led to an Award of Excellence by the UNESCO 2005 Asia-Pacific Heritage Awards for Culture Heritage Conservation Program in 2005.

Center right:
Looking out through one of the fan-shaped windows cut into the timbers along the sides of the bridge, the scenery conjures up a vision of a Chinese painting.

Far right:
Suffering from vandalism and lack of maintenance, the Houkeng Bridge had deteriorated substantially before its reconstruction began in 2001.

Dongguan Bridge
Yongchun, Fujian

The Huyang River in southern Fujian was long a vital link for the upland communities in Datian, Dehua, and Yongchun counties since it connected them with the great coastal port at Quanzhou. This river corridor, as well as others that poured from the mountains, played critical roles in the consolidation of Chinese control of the region and its economic transformation in the two and half centuries after 978. Although today it is eclipsed by better known ports such as Xiamen, Guangzhou, and Hong Kong, Quanzhou was China's key southeastern port during the Song dynasty, with international trade relations of enormous geographic scope. Overlaying the network of rivers was a lattice of byways and roads. Wherever the land routes crossed streams, there were fords, ferries, or bridges, sometimes one replacing another as travel and trade increased. Markets often were associated with these nodes.

Some 300 bridges are recorded to have been built in the broader Quannan region between 978 and 1275; many in remote areas never made it into the records (Clark, 1991: 95). As elsewhere, bridges were built by local officials, Buddhist sangha, individual monks, and private entrepreneurs. Today, there is little evidence of the old bridges in the mountainous areas, as important ones have been modernized and many more simply disappeared over time. It is remarkable that one grand bridge nearly 900 years old still stands.

The Dongguan (Eastern Pass) Bridge was built in 1145 during one of the most vigorous periods of bridge building during the early decades after the Song court retreated to a new capital at what is today Hangzhou in Zhejiang. A security force was stationed at the bridgehead as recently as the seventeenth century to guard against bandits and protect the bridge. There are details of regular maintenance and reconstruction of the Dongguan Bridge throughout the Ming and Qing dynasties.

With an overall length of 85 meters and width of 5 meters, the bridge is covered with a vividly painted wooden corridor. Four midstream granite piers lift the bridge as it crosses the Huyang River from north to south, which in spring especially is filled with torrents. Each of the stacked stone piers is approximately 15 meters high with one end pointed and tipped upward like the prow of a boat facing upstream. Atop each pier is a set of five layers of long granite slabs that function as cantilevered supports for a series of twenty-two enormous logs, each 16–18 meters long and 30–40 centimeters in diameter, depending on the variable distances between the piers. The bridge is the longest wooden beam bridge still standing in Fujian.

Although the entry to the bridge and the wooden framework are rather plain, the interior is richly ornamented with paintings. About midstream is a masonry structure set upon one of the piers with an uplifted roof like that of any temple. Within this structure is an elaborate altar to Guanyin, the Goddess of Mercy. The evidence of blackened beams and pungent incense underscores that this area continues to be a center for community life for those living in Dongmei village.

Above:
This view along the side of the Dongguan (Eastern Pass) Bridge shows clearly its four granite piers and the cantilevered stone slabs on top of them. Two sets of slanted wooden panels along each side of the bridge protect the wooden structure from rain while allowing for cross-ventilation.

Opposite below left and right:
The illuminated altar to the Goddess of Mercy, Guanyin, is protected with a sliding grate. Incense is placed in the vessel immediately in front of the altar as well as in a nearby censer.

Left:
Since the bridge is sometimes called the Tongxian (Passage of the Immortals) Bridge, tales of various immortals are painted on panels beneath the rafters along the full length of the corridor.

Covered Wooden Bridges   **245**

Yuwen Bridge
Taishun, Zhejiang

The Yuwen (Nourish Culture) Bridge is sited at a magi-cal spot in Zhouling township along the Hudie (Butter-fly) Stream, with rising hills on one side, ancient trees clinging to the other, well-worn boulders midstream, and a patina of green moss layering. The surrounding area is often shrouded in effervescent mist and clouds.

Built in 1839, the base of the Yuwen Bridge is a tightly compacted hemispheric stone arch with a diam-eter of 7.6 meters, similar to other stone bridges in the region. What is most distinctive about the bridge, how-ever, is its multitiered wooden corridor below a com-plicated tiered roof structure. The sides of the bridge are open since only the overhanging roof protects the wooden framework. The posts along each side are linked via a series of traditional lattice panels con-structed of sawn timber. From the inside, the wooden framework acts as a frame for the scenes outside.

With a length of 23 meters and width of 4 meters, the interior is divided into seven structural bays. Mid-way across the span, a wooden ladder leads to a loft on the second storey with a double-tiered flying eaves form similar to that found atop country temples. The extensive religious space on this second level, called the Wenchang Pavilion, enshrines the Daoist deity Imperial Sovereign Wenchang Di, who is said to be the "Promoter of Benevolence and Controller of Wealth Who Serves the Origin and Initiates Salvation." A compound deity, Wenchang is revered as a model of filial piety and benevolence, especially because of loyalty towards his mother, and as the regulator of appointments of officials. Popularly known to West-erners as the God of Literature, he is usually depicted wearing the robe of an official and holding a scepter.

Above left:
When approached from the stone-lined path dropping from the mountain, the Yuwen (Nourish Culture) Bridge appears set into a deep ravine.

Above:
Hugged by gnarled trees and washed by wisps of mist, the multistoried Yuwen Bridge commands its site.

Left:
Besides Wenchang, Tianlong, and Diya, myriad other Daoist and local deities are placed within niches in the second-level religious space.

Right:
Looking out from any vantage point within the bridge is a framed image of trees, rocks, and water.

Far right:
View of the intersection of posts, beams, purlins, braces, and rafters at a corner of the bridge.

DONG "WIND-AND-RAIN" BRIDGES

SANJIANG, GUANGXI

The Dong ethnic group, one of China's fifty-five minority nationalities, has been described as having an "architecture-based culture" in which life and built culture are inextricably interrelated (Ruan, 2006: 23–37). With a population of about 3 million, the Dong live in villages called *zhai* or "stockades" in the rugged region linking northern Guangxi, southern Guizhou, and southern Hunan provinces. In Dong villages, which usually straddle streams, several types of buildings stand as signature public structures arranged in well-defined compositions: altars or shrines, village gate, drum tower, opera stage, and "wind-and-rain bridges." While each of these Dong building types is distinctive individually, collectively they provide a striking picturesqueness in which buildings, agriculture, and the natural landscape are in harmony.

Any Dong building, whether a bridge, drum tower, or house, is usually built using timber from a single tree species called "eighteen-year China fir" that matures in about eighteen years. Trees of this type are frequently planted when a child is born, with the expectation that over eighteen years—as the child matures to the age of marriage—the trees will have matured to a size suitable for building a home for the newlywed couple. A multistoried drum tower built of fir is viewed as an "umbrella" to shelter villagers. When a drum tower is destroyed by fire or accident, the Dong raise the trunk of a large fir tree on the drum tower site as a transitory replacement before a new one is built.

"Wind-and-rain bridges"—called *fengyu qiao* in Chinese—are especially noteworthy for their wooden covered superstructures that allow the buildings to serve both as a covered corridor as well as a pavilion for leisure. In terms of structure and overall composition, a wind-and-rain bridge is constructed of four parts: stone piers, an inverse pyramidal frame made of massive logs held together by tenons that serves as cantilevered support, an open or semienclosed corridor (sometimes with a shrine inside), and a roof.

Left:
Sited at a picturesque location, the Batuan Bridge is unique in that it has two separate corridors, one for animals and one for pedestrians.

Right:
From the main road to reach Ma'an village, one needs to descend steps before climbing others that lead to the Chengyang Bridge.

The five pavilions which dominate the profile of the Chengyang Bridge across the Linxi River in Ma'an village, are reminiscent of Dong drum towers and include a 7.8-meter-tall central structure in a hexagonal shape. Each of the flanking lower pair of pavilions is 7 meters in height, while the outer ones with double-sloped roofs are 6.5 meters tall.

Above:
The upturned eaves of the pavilions of any Dong bridge are painted with colorful geometric shapes.

Usually, each pier is crowned with a pavilion with a quadrangular or hexagonal roof with multitiered eaves. Each pavilion not only adds weight at locations needed to stabilize the overall structure, but also contributes to the beauty of the bridge. The entire bridge structure—except for the stone piers—is built of timber without nails using mortise-and-tenoned joinery. In connecting a village with the world beyond, each wind-and-rain bridge is located either at the "head" of a village—that is, an upstream area—and/or at the "tail" of the village downstream. Bridges are not commonly built near the center of a village since such a location is considered a "belly" that must be avoided in order to prevent pestilence. Whenever a bridge is located at a more central location, it is usually because of a need to link propitious "dragon veins."

Yet, Dong wind-and-rain bridges serve more than to span a stream. Each is a public structure that offers shelter for weary travelers and nearby farmers, protecting them from the elements—wind and rain. In addition, it is to the bridge that villagers retreat on hot or rainy days while couples look for romance under the moonlight or in darkness. As with many other covered bridges elsewhere in China, there are altars to gods, such as Guan Di, also called Guan Gong, a compassionate, courageous, and virtuous general. Guandi, who is shown as a red-faced armor-clad warrior with a long lush beard, is worshipped

in many incarnations: a Daoist guardian deity, a Buddhist bodhisattva charged with protecting the dharma, as well as an heroic historic figure thought to be just and righteous. In southern China, moreover, many view Guandi as an alternative God of Wealth in that he is capable of providing blessings to those who are upright while protecting them from those who are dishonest. Bridges, like other buildings, are usually sited carefully using *fengshui* principles, since villagers believe that a properly located bridge can protect the wealth of a village from being drained away by its streams.

In three rural townships in the Sanjiang district of Guangxi, there are 112 wind-and-rain bridges alone. Among the most representative and clearly the most famous is the Chengyang Bridge, also called the Yongji Bridge, which spans the Linxi River in Ma'an village. Constructed between 1912 and 1924 with the support of villagers living in eight *zhai*, the bridge is 77.76 meters long, 11.52 meters high, and 3.75 meters wide, with five piers and four 17.3-meter-wide openings. In 1953, the bridge was recognized as a provincial heritage site and in 1982 was granted national heritage status. Sadly, much of the bridge was destroyed in 1983 because of flood, but this disaster spurred extensive renovation that, even after nearly a quarter century, has given the Chengyang Bridge a strikingly new, if not weathered, look.

Three cantilevered layers of fir logs—a series of projecting horizontal beams some 7–8 meters in length—are laid longitudinally across the top of each of the five stone piers each measuring 2.5 meters wide by 8.2 meters long. Between the four levels of cantilevered logs, which are held firmly in place by tenoned timbers, are placed thin spacer logs that together not only stabilize the support but also give the substructure some degree of flexibility. These then support a continuous overhanging wooden corridor built of interlocked columns and beams that divide the interior into nineteen bays or *jian*. Five pavilions with stacked flying eaves rising above the five piers endow the bridge with a distinctive architectural rhythm.

Arranged symmetrically, the central pavilion on the bridge is the tallest at 7.8 meters. Those on both sides of it are 7 meters tall, while the two outer pavilions rise 6.5 meters above the bridge. The middle, taller pavilion is topped with a hexagonal structure, reminiscent of a drum tower, while the two pavilions adjacent to it have pyramidal hipped roofs with four slopes. The end pavilions have five-layer rectangular gambrel roofs—double-sloped roofs with the upper slopes of a lesser pitch than the lower ones. All of the roofs are covered with gray tiles of the sort found on dwellings and temples. Wherever there are eaves, just as on similar drum towers, one finds colorful painted

Opposite above:
Because of the care taken in the siting of a Dong bridge, as in this case with the Chengyang Bridge, beautiful scenery greets anyone sitting on one of the benches inside.

Top:
This view of the midstream piers that support the Chengyang Bridge reveals the interconnected nature of the overall wooden framework.

Above:
The layers of cantilevered fir logs include a level of movable spacer logs joined by tenoned joints, which give the bridge a degree of flexibility.

Top:
The Batuan Bridge, built in 1910 across a narrow section of the Miao Stream in the Sanjiang district of Guangxi, is 150 meters long and has three pavilions atop it.

Left:
This shrine on the Batuan Bridge includes two images of what are popularly called "Door Gods" or *menshen*.

Above:
The principal corridor of the Batuan Bridge is defined by a wooden framework of substantial proportions, including a high ridge line, benches in broader extensions along the side, and a large altar, currently empty of any deities and ritual paraphernalia.

Above:
At grade level on the left is
the lower separate entrance
that leads to a corridor for
animals to cross the Batuan
Bridge. Pedestrians leaving
the village usually climb the
stone steps on the right to
reach the corridor on the
upper level.

Right:
When viewed from below,
the junctures of the upturned
eaves of the piled tile roofs
reveal a pleasing rhythm of
textures, shapes, and colors.

images of mountains, rivers, flowers, birds, fish, and other animals. Looking into the upper reaches of the central hexagonal pavilion from the inside of the bridge, one sees clearly a sunken coffered ceiling.

With the coming of domestic tourism to the Sanjiang region, the Chengyang Bridge no longer bears the traffic it once did, in as much as a modern bridge has been constructed near by to carry vehicular and animal traffic. Today, the bridge is open only to pedestrians. While visiting pedestrians are able to sit on the wood plank benches along the covered corridor to enjoy the breeze, they must also mix with the countless villagers who use the bridge to sell homespun fabrics and embroidered Dong-style clothing.

While the Chengyang Bridge is outstanding for its size and ornamentation, the Batuan Bridge stands out because of its two separate corridors, a lower narrow one 1.8 meters wide at grade level, through which animals can be led across, and an upper wider one 3.9 meters wide, which is reached by stone steps, for pedestrians and sitters. Built in 1910 as a unique double-passage structure, the 50-meter-long span rises above a narrow section of the Miao Stream at high locations along its bank. While the stream appears much of the time to be shallow and sluggish, the water is far from languishing during late spring and summer as can be attested by the significant accumulations of rubble stone and gravel along its banks as well as the

well-worn nearby rock surfaces. Stone abutments on both ends extend well beyond the stream's bank in order to offer supplementary support to the massive cantilevered logs that reach toward the single mid-stream pier. Three hipped-roof pavilions, the central one being somewhat taller and more elaborate than the matching pair on each side, are symmetrically placed above the linear roofline, highlighting the covered corridor and at the same time mimicking the roofs of village houses in the distance. Few outsiders visit the Batuan Bridge since it is located in a difficult-to-reach village. The centrality and significance of the bridge to villagers are attested to by the steady traffic

Above and left:
When encountered in the summer of 2006, this newly constructed bridge had nothing that indicated its name or the facts of its construction. As seen here, its raw wooden framework exposes many facets of the carpentry necessary for its construction atop a prestressed concrete substructure.

of humans and animals across it as they travel, often daily, between their homes and stables in the *zhai* and the terraced fields on the nearby hillslopes and in the valley bottoms.

Although there is no evidence remaining of which deities were once worshipped within the bridge, along a narrow lane there are two nearby active temples, the Huoshen Shrine and the

Left:
With sawhorses left in place, it is clear that the carpenters expect to return for additional carpentry work.

Above:
This view up through the center pavilion reveals the markings of recent rituals during the raising of its ridge beam.

Above:
Carpenters and villagers in this Dong village in Sanjiang county work together on an auspicious day to add bays to the corridor bridge as well as to raise the ridge beam as part of the central pavilion.

Far left:
Using a common saw, this carpenter cuts a piece of timber to the size needed for the wooden framework of the new bridge.

Left:
The carpenters here are fitting together the mortise-and-tenoned joinery that gives strength to the various timber components.

Far left:
In celebration of the building of a new dwelling and a new covered wind-and-rain bridge near by, as with weddings and funerals, women feast separately from men.

Left:
Ready for roasting, this large pig was paraded throughout the village on the day work was being completed on the new wind-and-rain bridge.

Below center:
Here, the carpenter is using his short-handled tool with a broad blade to fashion shims for the mortise-and-tenoned structure.

Below right:
The loop at the top can be attached to a pole so that the carpenter can carry his tools on his shoulder.

Bottom:
Villagers take a respite from their work to watch a friendly competition between two water buffalos in the stream channel. The timber components for the bridge lie in the background.

Above left:
Situated in the rear of Ma'an village, this small wooden covered bridge was constructed on a prestressed concrete foundation.

Left:
Each of the several altars found along the corridor in the Helong Bridge in Linxi village, just behind Ma'an village, contains statues carved from blocks of wood.

Above:
The Bajiang Bridge, Sanjiang county, was reconstructed some 400 meters downstream from its original location in order to enhance the village's *fengshui*.

Right:
With the drum tower in the distance reflected in the stream, the comparatively plain Helong Bridge serves residents in Linxi village.

Wenchang Palace. Both of these structures include within them several additional deities other than the dominant Daoist ones: Huoshen, known as the Fire Spirit or Fire God, is worshipped widely in China as is Imperial Sovereign Wenchang, who is sometimes referred to as the God of Literature.

In general, townspeople and villagers enter small religious facilities like these as and when the spirit moves them or if there is a request that needs to be made. Trays of food as well as fragrant incense and lighted tapers are regularly placed before images of the deities, offered usually with a prayer. A woman attendant is ready to help any of the supplicants, especially if there is a request to shake a tube of bamboo slips in pursuit of a prognostication.

BIBLIOGRAPHY

Attiret, Jean-Denis, *A Particular Account of the Emperor of China's Gardens near Pekin*, London: R. Dodsley, 1752.

Bian Li, *Huizhou gu qiao: Tongxiang shijie de lu* (Old Bridges of Huizhou: The Road Towards the World), Shenyang: Liaoning renmin chubanshe, 2002.

Bird, Isabella L. [Mrs. J. F. Bishop], *Chinese Pictures: Notes on Photographs Made in China*, London: Cassell, 1900.

_____, *The Yangtze River and Beyond: An Account of Journeys in China, Chiefly in the Province of Sze Chuan and Among the Man-Tze of the Somo Territory*, London: John Murray, 1899.

Boxer, C. R., *South China in the Sixteenth Century*, London: The Hakluyt Society, 1953.

Brown, Arthur Judson, *New Forces in Old China: An Inevitable Awakening*, New York: Fleming H. Revell Company, 1904.

Chen Congzhou, *Guangyuan* (On Chinese Bridges), Shanghai: Tongji University Press, 1985.

Chen Congzhou and Pan Hongxuan (eds.), *Shaoxing shi qiao* (Shaoxing Stone Bridges), Shanghai: Shanghai kexue jishu chubanshe, 1986.

Clark, Hugh, *Community, Trade, and Networks: Southern Fujian Province from the Third to the Thirteenth Century*, Cambridge: Cambridge University Press, 1991.

Coyne, Peter, "The Ancient Bridges of Soochow," *Arts of Asia*, 18, 1988, pp. 174–82.

_____, "The Artistry of China's Traditional Bridges," *Oriental Art*, 36(2), 1990, pp. 83–91.

_____, "Bridges of Imperial China," *Arts of Asia*, 21(1), 1991, pp. 95–103.

_____, "Carpenters of the Rainbow," *Archaeology*, 45(2), 1992, pp. 32–6.

_____, "China's Historic Bridges: An Enduring Link with the Past," *Arts of Asia*, 19, 1989, pp. 109–15.

Dai Zhijian, *Zhongguo langqiao* (China's Covered Bridges), Fuzhou: Fujian renmin chubanshe, 2005.

Flath, James A., "Setting Moon and Rising Nationalism: Lugou Bridge as Monument and Memory," *International Journal of Heritage Studies*, 10(2), 2004, pp. 175–92.

Fugl-Meyer, Helge, *Chinese Bridges*, Shanghai: Kelly and Walsh Ltd, 1937.

Gordon, Charles George, *Letters of General C. G. Gordon to His Sister, M. A. Gordon*, London, New York: Macmillan and Co., 1888.

Hake, A. Egmont, *The Story of Chinese Gordon*, New York: R. Worthington, 1884.

Institute of the History of Natural Sciences, Chinese Academy of Sciences (comp.), *Ancient China's Technology and Science*, Beijing: Foreign Languages Press, 1983.

Keswick, Maggie, *The Chinese Garden: History, Art and Architecture*, Cambridge: Harvard University Press, 2003.

Kieschnick, John, *The Impact of Buddhism on Chinese Material Culture*, Princeton: Princeton University Press, 2003.

Knapp, Ronald G., "Bridge on the River Xiao," *Archaeology*, 41(1), 1988, pp. 48–54.

_____, "Chinese Bridges," *Orientations*, 15(6), 1984, pp. 36–47.

_____, *Chinese Bridges*, New York: Oxford University Press, 1993.

_____, "Rainbows and Centipedes: The Search for China's 'Lost' Bridges," *Orientations*, 39(4), 2008.

_____, "Siting and Situating a Dwelling: *Fengshui*, House Building Rituals, and Amulets," in Ronald G. Knapp and Kai-Yin Lo (eds.), *House Home Family: Living and Being Chinese*, Honolulu: University of Hawai'i Press, 2005, pp. 99–137.

Lau, D. K., *Mencius*, New York: Penguin Books, 1984.

Liang Ssu-ch'eng [Liang Sicheng], "Open Spandrel Bridges of Ancient China—1: The An-chi Ch'iao at Chao Chou, Hopei," *Progressive Architecture, Pencil Points*, 19, 1938, pp. 25–32.

_____, "Shi langan jianshuo" (Brief Examination of Stone Balustrades), in *Liang Sicheng wenji* (Collected Writings of Liang Sicheng), Vol. 2, Beijing: Zhongguo jianzhu gongye chubanshe, 1984.

Little, Mrs Archibald, *Intimate China: The Chinese as I Have Seen Them*, London: Hutchinson & Co., 1899.

Liu Heping, "Painting and Commerce in Northern Song Dynasty China, 960–1126," Ph.D Dissertation, Yale University, 1997.

Liu Jie and Shen Weiping, *Taishun langqiao* (Lounge Bridges in Taishun), Shanghai: Shanghai People's Fine Arts Publishing House, 2005.

_____, *Xiangtu Shouning* (Bucolic Shouning), Beijing: Xinhua chubanshe, 2007.

Luo Zhewen, Liu Wenyuan, and Liu

Chunying (eds.), *Zhongguo ming qiao* (Famous Bridges of China), Tianjin: Baihua wenyi chubanshe, 2001.

Mao Yisheng, *Bridges in China: Old and New*, Beijing: Foreign Languages Press, 1978.

Mao Yisheng (chief ed.), *Zhongguo gu qiao jishu shi* (A Technological History of Ancient Chinese Bridges), Beijing: Beijing chubanshe, 1986.

Ministry of Communications of the People's Republic of China, *Zhongguo qiao pu* (A Guide to Chinese Bridges), Beijing: Waiwen chubanshe, 2003.

Mock, Elizabeth B., *The Architecture of Bridges*, New York: The Museum of Modern Art, 1949.

Morris, Edwin, *The Gardens of China: History, Art, and Meaning*, New York: Scribner, 1983.

Needham, Joseph, *Science and Civilization in China: Physics and Physical Technology*, Vol. 4, Part III, Cambridge: Cambridge University Press, 1971.

Neville-Hadley, Peter, "'Darkest China' Hides Gorgeous Surprises," *North Shore News*, March 15, 2004.

Ningde shi wenhua yu chubanji (Cultural and Publishing Department of Ningde City), *Ningde shi hongliang shi mugou langwuqiao* (Wooden Covered Rainbow-style Bridges of Ningde City), Beijing: Kexue chubanshe, 2006.

Olivová, Lucie, "Forgotten Bridges in Southern Hebei: Dulin qiao and Shan qiao," *Bulletin of the Museum of Far Eastern Antiquities*, 75, 2003, pp. 220–42.

Pan Hongxuan, *Jiangnan gu qiao* (Old Bridges of Jiangnan), Hangzhou: Zhejiang sheying chubanshe, 1999.

_____, *Zhongguo de gu ming qiao* (Famous Bridges of China), Shanghai: Xinhua shudian, 1985.

Qiaoliang shihua (History of Bridges), Shanghai: Shanghai kexue jishu chubanshe, 1979.

Ruan, Xing, *Allegorical Architecture: Living Myth and Architectonics in Southern China*, Honolulu: University of Hawaii Press, 2006.

Ruitenbeek, Klaas, *Building & Carpentry in Late Imperial China: A Study of the Fifteenth Century Carpenter's Manual Lu Ban Jing*, Leiden: E. J. Brill, 1993.

Service, Grace, *Golden Inches: The China Memoir of Grace Service*, Berkeley: University of California Press, 1989.

Silbergeld, Jerome, "Beyond Suzhou: Region and Memory in the Gardens of Sichuan," *The Art Bulletin*, 86(2), 2004, pp. 202–27.

Siren, Osvald, *Gardens of China*, New York: The Ronald Press, 1949.

So, Billy K. L., *Prosperity, Region, and Institutions in Maritime China: The South Fukien Pattern, 946–1368*, Cambridge: Harvard University Press, 2000.

Tang Huancheng, *Zhongguo gudai qiaoliang* (Ancient Chinese Bridges), Beijing: Wenwu chubanshe, 1987.

Tang Huancheng and Lu Jiaxi (eds.), *Zhongguo kexue jishu shi: Qiaoliang juan* (History of China's Science and Technology: Bridges), Beijing: Kexue chubanshe, 2000.

Wang, Joseph Cho, *The Chinese Garden*, New York: Oxford University Press, 1998.

Wiens, Herold J., "The Shu Tao or Road to Szechwan," *Geographical Review*, 39(4), 1949, pp. 584–604.

Wong, Young-tsu, *A Paradise Lost: The Imperial Garden Yuanming Yuan*, Honolulu: University of Hawaii Press, 2001.

Xue Yiquan, *Jiedu langqiao* (Reading Covered Bridges), Beijing: Zhongguo minzu sheying yishu chubanshe, 2005.

Zhang Huimin and Zhou Yusheng, *Shanghai de qiao* (Bridges of Shanghai), Shanghai: Huadong shifan daxue chubanshe, 2000.

Zhonggong Qingyuan xian weiyuanhui xuanchuan bu (Propaganda Office of the Chinese Communist Party, Qingyuan county), *Zhongguo langqiao zhi xiang—Qingyuan* (China's Covered Bridges Country—Qingyuan), Hangzhou: Xiling yinshe chubanshe, 2007.

Below:
Constructed to replicate the famed rainbow bridge found in Zhang Zeduan's twelfth-century *Qingming shanghe tu* painting, this red timber arched bridge, which crosses a canal in Jinze watertown in the suburbs of Shanghai, is a modern structure at a smaller scale.

INDEX

ACKNOWLEDGMENTS

It has been wonderful collaborating again with A. Chester Ong on a book that features his stunning yet sensitive photography. Upon completion of our award-winning *Chinese Houses* (2005), we traveled together four times to China to document not only some of the country's best-known bridges but also to search out and photograph little-known gems that exist in rather astounding numbers. The challenge to a photographer of Chinese houses is capturing light where often there is little and making three-dimensional spaces meaningful. Photographing old bridges is no less daunting since many are in quite remote areas, with slippery approaches, muddy stream bottoms, and fickle backgrounds. We hope that we have succeeded in presenting the bridges as more than mere structures since their cultural significance is equally important. On two trips we were assisted by either my son Jeff or daughter Larissa, who helped with heavy equipment and offered sometimes unexpected perspectives on what we were doing. Besides having the opportunity to venture into rarely visited areas of China, both also had a chance to come to a better understanding of what their father does when he is in the field. These trips have left many fine memories and interesting tales for each of us.

As is often the case, this book has undergone a number of significant conceptual changes over the past three years as it has developed. Chester and I embarked on the project without a contract in hand, convinced that his stunning photography and my text, once completed, would eventually convince a publisher of the merit of a book on a little-appreciated topic. We were delighted in due course when Eric Oey, CEO and Publisher of the Periplus Group, offered us a contract to present the project as a companion volume to *Chinese Houses*. At the time, we were not able to anticipate the significant role Eric would eventually play in bringing the book to its current form. Working on the design with Levi Christin in his Singapore office, Eric totally immersed himself in the manuscript and worked tirelessly in selecting images from sometimes chaotic thumbnails, as well as preparing layouts that were frequently revised to optimize the images and text. The book clearly has grown in size and beauty because of his active concern and involvement. We owe special thanks also to Noor Azlina Yunus, Senior Editor at Tuttle/Periplus in Malaysia, who not only offered helpful advice in the early stages of the manuscript but returned from retirement to edit the text. Just as with *Chinese Houses*, her careful work has enhanced what the reader has in hand.

We are especially proud to present the first full treatment in English of China's remarkable covered bridges, especially the extraordinary woven timber arch-beam bridges that until recently were essentially unknown even in China. The friendship and guidance of Liu Jie, a young scholar at Shanghai's Jiaotong University, was critical in helping us make arrangements to undertake three excursions to northern Fujian and southern Zhejiang, often over very difficult mountain roads. Indeed, it is principally due to him that the Chinese public and scholars have come to learn of these bridges. His energy and selflessness are exemplary. We appreciate his introducing us also to an even younger covered bridge enthusiast, Xue Yichuan, who tirelessly photographed the full process of building a covered bridge over a 26-month period in 2004–6. Fourteen of his unique photographs appear in Part II.

It was Peter Bol who helped clarify for me the need to see bridges as nodes in economic and cultural networks. His continuing work with Liu Jie and Wu Songdi to understand the spatial relationships relating bridges, stone pathways, lineage halls, and settlements generally is not only important academic work, it contributes as well to fostering local appreciation of cultural heritage in China and spurring conservation of structures facing destruction. Chester and I deeply appreciate Peter's willingness to write a Foreword to *Chinese Bridges* since his generous words will also help raise awareness of bridges as important aspects of China's architectural heritage.

Special thanks are due to Elizabeth Brotherton, an art historian colleague specializing in China at SUNY New Paltz, who discussed with me many suggestions of fine paintings with bridges in them that I could review for possible inclusion in the book. I hope she will be pleased with the ones I have chosen. I am also grateful for the assistance of Freda Murck in Beijing, whose contacts made it possible to obtain high-quality digital images of two important paintings.

I deeply appreciate the cooperation of reproduction specialists and rights gatekeepers for permitting the use of valuable art images from their collections, especially the Academy of Natural Sciences, Philadelphia; the British Museum, London; the Dorsky Museum of Art, State University of New York at New Paltz; the Freer Gallery of Art and the Arthur M. Sackler Gallery, Smithsonian Institution, Washington; the Metropolitan Museum of Art, New York; the Museum of Chinese History, Beijing; the Palace Museum, Beijing; and the Shanghai Museum.

The following list acknowledges the sources of all illustrations, where these are known, other than those taken by A. Chester Ong of extant bridges. The relevant page numbers are given in bold.

a=above; b=below; c=center; l=left; r=right

Front endpaper: Wang Hui (Chinese, 1632–1717) and assistants, *The Kangxi Emperor's Southern Tour, Scroll Three: Ji'nan to Mount Tai,* Qing dynasty (1644–1911), datable to 1691–8, handscroll, ink and color on silk, 67.8 x 1393.8 cm. The Metropolitan Museum of Art. Purchase, The Dillon Fund Gift, 1979 (1979.5). Image © The Metropolitan Museum of Art, New York.

Back endpaper: *Zhaozhou Stone Bridge With Baxian [Eight Immortals], Lu Ban, and Others Crossing It*, ca. 2000, woodcut on paper, 30.1 x 45.4 cm. Courtesy of Samuel Dorsky Museum of Art, State University of New York at New Paltz. Gift of Ronald G. Knapp, 2005.068.002.

p. 8: *Portuguese Ambassador Presents His Credentials at the Imperial Palace.* © The Trustees of the British Museum.

p. 12: *Landscape: Mountain Gorge, a Stream, Houses, and People*, Qing dynasty (1644–1911), hanging scroll, ink and color on silk, ht 179.8, w 61.0 cm. Gift of Charles Lang Freer, F1909.167. © Freer Gallery of Art, Smithsonian Institution, Washington, DC.

p. 19ar: Zhu Xieyuan, *Tieqiao zhi shu* (Record of the Iron Suspension Bridge), 17th century.

p. 20b: Zhang Zeduan, *Qingming shanghe tu* (Going Up River During the Qingming Festival), 11th–12th century. © Palace Museum, Beijing.

p. 21a: Shitao (1642–1707), *Waters Rise in Spring.* © Shanghai Museum.

p. 23: *Emperor Minghuang's Journey to Sichuan*, painting, Ming dynasty, after Qiu Ying (1494–1552). Purchase F1993.4. © Freer Gallery of Art, Smithsonian Institution, Washington, DC.

p. 31a: Bamboo Pontoon Bridge, Western China. © Special Collections, Yale Divinity School Library, New Haven, Connecticut.

p. 31b: Helge Fugl-Meyer, *Chinese Bridges*, Shanghai: Kelly and Walsh Ltd, 1937, p. 48.

p. 32b: Photographed by A. Chester Ong at a temple near the Bei'an Bridge, Shexian, Anhui.

p. 35a: Shitao (Zhu Ruoji) (1642–1707), *Drunk in Autumn Woods*, Qing dynasty (1644–1911), ca. 1702, hanging scroll, ink and color on paper, image 161 x 70.5 cm, overall mounting 273.1 x 84.8 cm, overall with knobs 273.1 x 93.7 cm. The Metropolitan Museum of Art, Purchase, Gift of John M. Crawford Jr, 1987 (1987.202). Image © The Metropolitan Museum of Art, New York.

p. 35b: Arthur Hacker, *China Illustrated: Western Views of the Middle Kingdom*, Singapore: Tuttle Publishing, 2004, p. 47.

p. 36a: Isabella L. Bird [Mrs J. F. Bishop], *Chinese Pictures: Notes on Photographs Made in China*, London: Cassell, 1900, p. 47.

p. 37b: Mrs. Archibald Little, *Intimate China: The Chinese as I Have Seen Them*, London: Hutchinson and Co., 1899, p. 47.

p. 40a: *Zhaozhou Stone Bridge With Baxian [Eight Immortals], Lu Ban, and Others Crossing It*, ca. 2000, woodcut on paper, 30.1 x 45.4 cm. Courtesy of Samuel Dorsky Museum of Art, State University of New York at New Paltz. Gift of Ronald G. Knapp, 2005.068.002.

p. 40c: Photographed by A. Chester Ong at an onsite exhibition at the Zhaozhou Bridge.

p. 40b: Photographed by A. Chester Ong at an onsite exhibition at the Zhaozhou Bridge.

p. 46b: Shahe Bridge, Library of Congress Prints and Photographs Division, Washington, DC. Reproduction Number LC-USZ62-54320.

pp. 48–9b: Zhang Zeduan, *Qingming shanghe tu* (Going Up River During the Qingming Festival), 11th–12th century. © Palace Museum, Beijing.

p. 48a: NOVA program "China Bridge," originally broadcast on February 29, 2000, as part of the series *Secrets of Lost Empire.* NOVA Online is produced for PBS by the WGBH Science Unit.

p. 50b: Longitudinal elevation view of the Santiao Bridge, Taishun county, Zhejiang, in Liu Jie and Shen Weiping, *Taishun langqiao* (Lounge Bridges in Taishun), Shanghai: Shanghai People's Fine Arts Publishing House, 2005, p. 111.

pp. 51a: Wo Bridge, photograph taken by US Army Officers Lt. Col. Ilya Tolstoy and Capt. Brooke Dolan, 1942–3. ANS Archives Coll. 64CII(b) T37 #22. © The Academy of Natural Sciences, Philadelphia, Pennsylvania.

p. 51bl: Isabella L. Bird [Mrs. J. F. Bishop], *The Yangtze Valley and Beyond: An Account of Journeys in China, Chiefly in the Province of Sze Chuan and Among the Man-Tze of the Somo Territory*, London: John Murray, 1899, p. 107.

p. 51br: Isabella L. Bird [Mrs. J. F. Bishop], *Chinese Pictures: Notes on Photographs Made in China*, London: Cassell, 1900, p. 51.

p. 58a: Arthur Hacker, *China Illustrated: Western Views of the Middle Kingdom*, Singapore: Tuttle Publishing, 2004, p. 131.

p. 58c: Library of Congress Prints and Photographs Division, Washington, DC. Reproduction Number LC-USZ62-56122.

p. 61b: Mrs. Archibald Little, *Intimate China: The Chinese as I Have Seen Them*, London: Hutchinson and Co., 1899, p. 389.

pp. 68–9: *Feiduo Luding qiao* (Capturing the Luding Bridge), Leiden University International Institute of Social History, Stefan R. Landsberger Collection http://www.iisg.nl/~landsberger

pp. 70, 73bl/b/r, 74–5 (all): Photographs of bridge building and rituals taken in Taishan county, Zhejiang, used with the permission of Xue Yichuan.

p. 71: *Lu Ban jing*, ca. 1600, as reproduced in Klaas Ruitenbeek, *Carpentry & Building in Late Imperial China: A Study of the Fifteenth Century Carpenter's Manual Lu Ban Jing*, Leiden: E. J. Brill, 1993, p. 113.

p. 86b: Iron Chain Bridge Over the Dadu River in Luding County. © China Internet Information Center.

p. 87l: Rolf Müller, permission granted under the terms of the GNU Free Documentation License.

p. 87br: *South China Morning Post, post-magazine*, September 16, 2007, p. 22.

p. 98a: Zhang Bao, *Fan cha tu* , 1831; reprinted Beijing: Beijing guji chubanshe, 1988.

p. 102–3: *Mid-nineteenth Century View of Kunming Lake*, OA 1948.5.8.03. © The Trustees of the British Museum.

p. 106b: Osvald Siren, *The Imperial Palaces of Beijing*, Paris: G. Van Oest, 1926, Pl. 205.

p. 107b: Photographed by A. Chester Ong at an onsite exhibition at the Yuanming Yuan.

p. 109a: W. A. P. Martin, *A Cycle of Cathay: or, China, South and North*, New York: F. H. Revell, 1897, p. 244.

p. 112b: E. J. Hardy, *John Chinaman at Home: Sketches of Men, Manners and Things in China*, London: T. F. Unwin, 1906, p. 99.

p. 118: *Lugou yunfa tu* (Transporting Logs at the Lugou Bridge), painting, Yuan period, © Museum of Chinese History, Beijing.

p. 119: Gao Jin, *Nanxun shengdian* (Grandeur of the Qianlong Emperor's Southern Expedition), 1771; reprinted Taibei: Wenhai chubanshe, 1971.

p. 161a: Qian Songyan, *Canals and Bridges in the Jiangnan Region*, painting, 1963, 52.8 x 35.7 cm, in *Zhongguo Meishu nianjian* (Chinese Art Annual), Guilin: Guangxi meishu chubanshe, 1989.

p. 187a: Mrs. Archibald Little, *Intimate China: The Chinese as I Have Seen Them*, London: Hutchinson and Co., 1899, p. 395.

p. 214b: Photographed by A. Chester Ong from an onsite stele, Luoyang Bridge, Quanzhou, Fujian.

p. 215: *Building of the Wan'an (Luoyang) Bridge*, drawing, in *Wu Ying Wujiang chun tushuo*, ca. 1690; reproduced as a woodblock print in G. V. Ecke, "Zaytonische Granitbrücker: ihr Schmuck u. ihre Heiligtümer," *Sinica*, 6, 1931.

p. 228b: Transverse section of the Santiao Bridge, Taishun county, Zhejiang, in Liu Jie and Shen Weiping, *Taishun langqiao* (Lounge Bridges in Taishun), Shanghai: Shanghai People's Fine Arts Publishing House, 2005, p. 272.

p. 243br: The World Heritage Research Center, Peking University.

p. 259ar: Photograph used with the permission of Larissa L. Mentzer.